Learning Unplugged

Learning Unplugged

Using Mobile Technologies for Organizational Training and Performance Improvement

Diane Gayeski, Ph.D.

AMACOM

American Management Association

New York • Atlanta • Brussels • Buenos Aires • Chicago • London • Mexico City
San Francisco • Shanghai • Tokyo • Toronto • Washington, D.C.

Special discounts on bulk quantities of AMACOM books are
available to corporations, professional associations, and other
organizations. For details, contact Special Sales Department,
AMACOM, a division of American Management Association,
1601 Broadway, New York, NY 10019.
Tel.: 212-903-8316. Fax: 212-903-8083.
Web site: www.amacombooks.org

This publication is designed to provide accurate and authoritative
information in regard to the subject matter covered. It is sold with
the understanding that the publisher is not engaged in rendering
legal, accounting, or other professional service. If legal advice or other
expert assistance is required, the services of a competent professional
person should be sought.

Windows, Windows 95, Windows 98, Windows XP, Windows CE, Windows for Pocket PC, Microsoft Word, Excel, Outlook, and PowerPoint are either registered trademarks or trademarks of Microsoft Corporation in the United States and/or other countries.

Palm is a trademark and HotSync and Palm OS are registered trademarks of Palm, Inc.

Handspring, Visor, and Springboard are registered trademarks of Handspring, Inc.

Macromedia Flash and Dreamweaver are registered trademarks of Macromedia, Inc.

Symbian and all Symbian-based marks and logos are trademarks of Symbian Limited.

Adobe and Acrobat are trademarks or registered trademarks of Adobe Systems Incorporated in the U.S. and/or other countries.

RealAudio and RealJukebox are registered trademarks of RealNetworks.

JK

Library of Congress Cataloging-in-Publication Data

Gayeski, Diane M. (Diane Mary), 1953–
        Learning unplugged : using mobile technologies for organizational training and
    performance improvement / Diane Gayeski.
            p. cm.
        Includes index.
        ISBN 0-8144-7145-5
        1. Employees—Training of—Equipment and supplies. 2. Employees—Training of—Audio-
visual aids. 3. Instructional systems. I. Title: Mobile technologies for organizational training and
performance improvement. II. Title.

        HF5549.5.T7 G36 2002
        658.3'12404'02854678—dc21

                                                                                            2002018246

Printing number
10 9 8 7 6 5 4 3 2 1

Contents

Preface

I LOVE GIZMOS. Ever since I pressed my twelve-year-old nose against the control room window of the radio station that moved into my father's office building, I've been intrigued by communications media, especially new technologies. The "new" part for me has been portable video in the 1970s, interactive videotape and videodisc in the early 1980s, and CD-ROMs and the Internet in the 1990s. People often refer to me as a pioneer. To be sure, I've been the target of the arrows of crashed computers, sleepless nights, snake pits of wires, and rooms full of circuit boards and buttons with no directions. When I'd alpha-test new interactive products, my clients would half-jokingly tell me that if I found a bug, they would document it and call it a "feature."

A lot has changed over the past three decades, and there's always something new. That's why I wrote this book.

WHY I THINK WIRELESS PORTABLE COMPUTING DEVICES ARE THE NEXT BIG THING

❏ Smart training and communications professionals are positioning themselves as strategic workplace

performance improvement consultants. If you are one of these forward-looking leaders, you need to deliver information and instruction where the action is. That action is not always at a wired desktop, and it surely is not in a classroom or auditorium. From sales reps in the field through medical personnel on a hospital floor to production workers in a high-tech factory, many people who are essential to organizational success do not work at a desk. You've got to beam training, communication, advice, and documentation to their pockets, their cell phones, or maybe even to their wristwatches and eyeglasses.

It's happening now. My clients at the Ontario Gaming and Lottery Corporation are using personal digital assistants (PDAs) to record exemplary service encounters on the gaming floor to compile a best-practices scorecard. Another is using digital video on a personal digital assistant to provide training in a chip manufacturing plant. In the chapter in this book on GPS systems, you can read about how my clients at Maines Paper & Food Service are using global positioning devices and PDAs to improve delivery performance. For each organization, these are critical performance settings, and each of them is able to be supported by portable knowledge capture and dissemination devices.

❐ **Watch teenagers and smart executives.** What are their toys? MP3 players, PDAs, digital cameras, and GPS systems are everywhere. These folks are your audience and clients, whether you are in training and development, quality systems, communications, or information technologies.

❐ **Look at what today's headlines are saying about how critical functions are being supported.** Today's newsbytes from my online portal tell me that the U.S. military is using pocket computers to provide logistical support to field forces. From National Guard deployments in Kosovo, to Navy deployments in the Arabian Gulf, the military is using handheld computers to improve patient care, data collection, and inspection processes. Another press release reports that when a major utility implemented a wireless solution to communicate with its service crews, it increased the number of service calls it could handle each day by 32 percent. Yet another recent news story predicts that 90 percent of worldwide professionals and telecommuters will adopt wireless data solutions by 2005 to stay in touch. If you are not following these headlines, watch out, because somebody else is, and you'll be caught unprepared.

WHAT THIS BOOK WILL DO FOR YOU

This book encapsulates the kind of information I have recently been providing in my consulting engagements, workshops, and graduate courses. It is designed to tell you, in plain language, how you can adopt readily available, inexpensive, easy-to-use, miniature devices to provide information and communication support. You will see how a wide variety of organizations are using these devices right now, what it takes to design and produce software that runs on them, and what's in store for mobile technologies tomorrow.

WHAT YOU SHOULD DO: TODAY, THIS WEEK, AND THIS QUARTER

If you have not already done so, put mobile technologies in your budget and on your to-do list. It is likely that many end users of the kind of courses and information you are producing already have devices that you could be leveraging to increase learning, performance, collaboration, and revenue. Here is how to begin:

1. *Today:* Do a quick scan in your organization or among your clients. How are mobile devices like cell phones, personal digital assistants, or digital media devices such as music players and digital cameras already being used? Consider underserved audiences. Who are the critical performers, and how many of these people work in places that are not able to be served by computers, conventional telephones, or even bulky manuals? Imagine how their performance could be improved if you had an easy way to reach them as they work.

2. *This week.* Read this book. You may want to start with the chapters that feature devices that you know are already being deployed in your organization. Get ideas from the interviews featured in each chapter and check out the Web resources at the end of each chapter. Focus on one or two ideas that you could quickly prototype and show a real return on investment. Pass this book along to your key sponsors and clients with a sticky note highlighting sections that might inspire their support of a new initiative.

3. *This quarter.* Produce a prototype to show your executives or key clients and set a deadline for completion within the next six weeks or so. Consider getting help through a workshop or hiring outside experts to help you develop an application quickly. It should not cost a fortune; I have done prototypes within a week for most of the applications discussed in this book. These small devices *should* have small budgets and time frames. Get some feedback on your first effort, estimate the return on investment that you could anticipate for a full-scale deployment, and develop a vision and budget for mobile devices.

DO *I* ACTUALLY USE THIS STUFF?

You might wonder if I have the gizmos I write about in this book and, if so, how I use them. Fair enough.

I have a Handspring Visor with just about every plug-in module that you can buy: a digital camera, an MP3 player, an audio recorder, a GPS system, and a device that allows me to connect to an LCD projector to show electronic slides from it. I keep my calendar and contacts on it, get daily downloads of newspapers and business magazines, and even try to manage my diet and exercise with a nifty little software suite. I generally carry it around with the digital camera attached and use it like a visual notepad.

I have several digital cameras, both still and video, and I use them to grab shots for client projects when I am doing performance improvement projects or multimedia. I also use digital pictures to improve my ability to remember students' names and faces and to experiment with Web-based video-conferencing. I use the GPS to help me find my way around cities when I travel on consulting engagements and for conference presentations.

When Ithaca, New York, where I live, gets the proper type of cell phone service, I'll buy a smart cell phone that will allow me to browse the Web and connect to my e-mail. And when I find wearable computers in the petites' section of my favorite clothing stores, you can bet what my credit card bill will look like.

AND THE CREDITS ROLL

Writing a book is never a solo activity. My main source of enthusiasm and inspiration has been our chief technology officer at Gayeski Analytics, Evan Williams. Evan has tried out many of the gizmos I feature here, and he has helped me present workshops and write articles about them. The fact that he also happens to be my fifteen-year-old son makes this even more special. My mom, Alba Gayeski, may not be a technology fan, but she has cheerfully supported my interests in new media for my entire life. My clients are terrific sources of creativity. I tend to get called in when in-house professionals and other consultants have given up on solving a training or communications problem or when organizations are looking for the "next thing." These opportunities never fail to help me improve my own performance as well as my clients'. Finally, my colleagues and students at Ithaca College have been trusting supporters and receptive learners as I teach new concepts and applications that are often at the bleeding edge. Thanks to everybody.

CAN WE TALK?

I'd love to hear about your ideas, questions, challenges, and applications. Just call me on my PDA/cell phone/Dick Tracy watch. My e-mail is diane@dgayeski.com, and you can track my progress and latest thinking at www.dgayeski.com.

Learning
Unplugged

Cutting the Cord

The Mobile Revolution in Learning and Performance

ARE **YOU** truly ready for anytime, anywhere training? Can you help your organization deliver performance in an increasingly mobile and global environment? Are your courses, manuals, and employee newsletters available to everybody—from the factory worker who has no PC (and no place to put one), to the administrative assistant who moves around the facility to take meeting notes, to the sales force that spends most of its days in the car or customer offices, up through the CEO who likes to work from his corporate jet? Are you able to select faster, cheaper, newer devices not only for delivering training but for building your own toolkit in doing needs analysis, development, and assessment?

That's what this book is about: the use of small portable computing and communication devices for improving organizational learning and productivity. Although you may think that you're ahead of the curve if you're producing Web-based training, electronic performance support systems, or certification testing on your intranet, the heyday of wired computer systems has passed. Consider the following facts:

❑ There are about 50 million mobile workers in the United States alone.

❑ More than 400 million mobile phones were sold in 2000.

❑ Of the 9 million handheld computer units purchased in the past few years, 80 percent are synchronized to some corporate user's computer at work.

❑ Laptops and personal digital assistants now outnumber conventional desktop computers.

❑ Over two-thirds of the telephone numbers issued worldwide are for cellular phones.

It's estimated that by 2004, most office workers will have both cell phones and some type of mobile computing device. By then, according to *PC Magazine* (March 6, 2001), 61 million handheld computing devices will be in use compared to only 16.8 million desktop units. For less than the price of lunch for your project team, you can buy wristwatch audio players, a credit card–sized organizer that will store thousands of phone contacts and appointments, or a digital camera that can directly send its pictures via wireless e-mail, and browse the Web. New software systems can now turn your home or office PC into a mini-server that you can access from anywhere by using a variety of devices. You can be sitting in a traffic jam and download an audio file from your home PC and listen to it on your cell phone or use your personal digital assistant (PDA) to retrieve a user's manual from your office server while you're at a client site.

Get prepared for a new set of tools. The array of technologies can seem mind-boggling, and the technological standards are yet to be determined by the marketplace. But the good news is that using smart cell phones, pocket computers, and other gizmos is not only fun; it's easy and inexpensive. Let's get started.

WBT: WE'VE BEEN THERE (AND DONE THAT)

Using computers and other microprocessor devices for training is nothing new. I can remember unearthing teaching machines (filmstrip plus audio devices with pushbutton response units) that were already old when I was a graduate assistant in a university educational technology center in the mid-1970s. Large mainframe systems were being used for rudimentary computer-assisted instruction (CAI), and soon the Apple II and IBM PC computers made it possible to produce and deliver CAI on a desktop. The late 1980s and early 1990s brought multimedia power to these desktops and some degree of portability; my first portable computer, which I bought in 1982, was a Compaq that was the size of a substantial sewing machine! The ability to add video and audio through sound cards, videodiscs, and eventually CD-ROMs added to the available strategies for training.

One big limitation of all but the very earliest mainframe systems was that they were stand-alone. What seemed like an advantage in fact had serious drawbacks:

❐ It was easy for individual hard drives or diskettes to get corrupted or lost, and replacement was troublesome.

❐ It was difficult to update materials. One had to send out diskettes or CD-ROMs with new versions of training and documentation, and it was up to the individual end user to see that these updates were performed.

❐ Individualized learning was a solitary experience. Although these media were called "interactive," the real interactivity came between the user and a canned program, not with a live trainer or other classmates.

As we all know, the revolution of commerce and learning in the mid- to late 1990s was the Internet. Now, it is possible for users to access material that is updated on a host Web site, never having to worry about installing new programs. More important, people can actually interact with experts and cohorts. The Internet makes everybody (at least potentially) an information consumer and an information producer. Enter Web-based training (WBT), which many now consider to be state of the art in corporate training and higher education.

So, here we are with a seemingly powerful set of multimedia desktop tools with real-time connection to the real world. They sound like the ideal training, communication, and performance improvement devices for organizations. The problem is that while the training and corporate communication world was busy getting wired, the workplace was becoming mobile, flexible, and global. The Internet is great as long as you are sitting in your office or have a high-speed cable modem or digital subscriber line (DSL) connection at home. It is not so great when you are on the road, in a hotel room, or at a client site. And even the smallest laptop is a clumsy reference device when you are trying to troubleshoot a telephone system in a cramped equipment closet or attempting to develop specs for a new manufacturing facility while walking around a construction site.

Being tethered to an Internet line or being saddled with a laptop does not always work. But this is not the biggest limitation of typical Web-based training. Beyond the technical constraints, there is a philosophical mismatch between what typically passes as good WBT and what modern organizations need to improve performance. Most Web-based training is designed around courses that are designed, produced, and deployed by trainers and taken by learners. This idea of both the course and the learner ever being "done" is a fundamental mismatch with the kind of continuous improvement systems in place in most organizations. These courses mimic college curricula more than workplace performance improvement efforts. For example, is a course on leadership or negotiation ever really complete and up-to-date, and are learners ever completely through adding to their knowledge in this area?

Instead of courses, many training experts feel that we need "learning bytes"—little packages of content and job aids that people can access at the peak moment of teachability and performance enhancement. Ideally, learning would occur when and where people need it most and where it can most readily affect the success of their work. The information would be completely up-to-date and would be interactive in its style and content.

In order for communication, documentation, and training professionals to align their efforts more closely with the emerging landscape of the modern workplace, they need to make the following moves:

❏ From producing courses to developing learning and performance systems that "grow themselves"

❏ From managing certification to encouraging continuous learning and collaboration

❏ From developing curricula to building structures to capture and store knowledge bytes

❏ From teaching and telling to aiding performance

❏ From creating schedules and managing facilities to adapting to the schedules and locations of the workers

Let's think about where work really happens and how you can be prepared to serve your clients, sponsors, and key performers in a new way.

THE NEW WORK AND LEARNING ENVIRONMENT

I'm writing this on a flight from Dallas to Boston, having just put down a couple of crumpled business magazines. The pages are full of ads and stories featuring gizmos—handheld computers with dazzling color screens and built-in MP3 players, cell phones that call you with stock tips and enable you to trade online and then make reservations at a swanky restaurant to celebrate your latest deal, and a credit card–sized organizer that stores thousands of contacts and all your appointments for the next decade.

Sitting around me are your clients and customers—businesspeople on the go. As I walk through the first-class cabin, almost everybody is talking on cell phones. The man in front of me is paging through a slickly designed sales manual on his laptop. The woman across the aisle is blissfully listening to her MP3 player. And besides typing up this chapter on my laptop, I have a virtual arsenal of learning and performance improvement devices in my briefcase. In fact, they all fit in a case smaller than my cosmetic bag. I have a Handspring Visor, a palm-sized computing device that runs the familiar appointment organizer and contacts list. Docked onto the top of it is a small color digital camera; I use it to snap photos of interesting sights to e-mail to my son and capture images when I work at client sites. Also in that little bag are other snap-on tools:

- ❐ An MP3 player that is holding my personally selected mix of music and a couple of short interviews by business authors that I downloaded off the Web

- ❐ A global positioning system (GPS) device so I can find my way around Boston

- ❐ A digital audio recorder so I can capture some interviews for this book

Although I still travel with my trusty laptop, my Visor is always in my purse, even on short errands. The add-on devices are great boons to its usefulness, but even in its stripped-down state, the variety of software for it makes it a terrific device for improving my performance:

- ❐ I bought a $30 suite of software on the Web that allows me to manage my diet and exercise; I put in my weight-loss goals, and it calculates my calorie targets. Then I simply tap on a list of foods and types of activities (the list ranges from jogging through grooming to sleeping), and I can get immediate feedback on how to adjust my input and output to meet my goals. It's easy and the most effective behavior-modification program I have ever tried.

- ❐ I signed on to a free service that clips key articles and columns from a list of my favorite publications, including the *Economist* and the *New York Times*. Although it's no substitute for reading those magazines, it is less expensive and more convenient for getting the important trends I want to track.

❑ The address book, to-do list, and appointment book all "talk" to one another, which makes it easy to integrate data, make and reschedule appointments, and keep track of my obligations.

❑ I can sync all the information among my laptop, my Visor, and my customized "My Yahoo" portal, so that even if I do not have my pocket computer (or if its data get lost), I can access my schedule and important documents from any computer connected to the Internet.

Despite the predictions that technology would replace travel, the statistics have proved that quite the opposite has happened: We are traveling more than ever before. Because of technology, business and education relationships are easily forged across geographical distance; instead of looking for a school or supplier in your city, you are more likely to go shopping on the Web and find the one best tailored to your styles and needs. While some of these transactions take place online, people still need to meet face-to-face, and this is why the skies and highways are more crowded than ever before. We work and learn on airplanes, in hotel rooms, and even sitting by the pool on vacation.

The future of these devices for training and performance improvement is not just in the hands of jet-setting executives. With the rise in technology use for information and training, we have created somewhat of a gap between the haves and the have-nots. Not everybody has a computer at his or her desk; in fact, lots of people do not have desks. Until now, the only way to provide Web-based training or electronic performance support tools to them was to set up learning labs or public "bullpens." These solutions can work, but they do not capture people where they work and when they may have the most teachable moment.

So, what is the future of corporate learning and performance? It has being variously called m-learning (for mobile learning), persistent computing, wireless connectivity, or, as I call it, learning unplugged.

HONEY, I SHRUNK THE COMPUTER

What are these devices that are emerging as our new platform for personal performance? Actually, there is a small arsenal of devices that are basically the next generation of laptops, digital cameras, scanners, portable music players, and computer game devices. (In some cases, vendors are attempting to roll all of these into a single gadget.). Although this is a constantly moving target, it may be helpful to put this plethora of devices into somewhat of a taxonomy:

A personal digital assistant (Courtesy Casio)

Personal digital assistants (PDAs)

PDAs are handheld computers whose built-in software includes an address book, calendar, to-do list, and sometimes miniature versions of word processors, spreadsheets, and e-mail clients. There are two major operating system platforms: Palm OS (Palm Pilots and Handspring Visors) and Windows CE (HP Jornada, Compaq iPAQ).

An MP3 player
(Courtesy SonicBlue)

MP3 players

These are the next-generation Walkman Players, but instead of playing cassettes or CDs, they play back digital audio files. The files are typically downloaded from the Web or "ripped" (duplicated) from your own CDs using a conventional computer. Then they are downloaded into the MP3 player using a simple cable. You listen to files through a headset or adapter that lets you play it through your car radio.

MVC-CD200 CD Mavica
Digital camera (Courtesy
Sony Electronics, Inc.)

Digital text, audio, still picture, and video capture devices

A plethora of devices lets you capture text, pictures, audio, and motion video. Some of these are stand-alone devices, and some plug into PDAs. These allow you to create materials for training or documentation, and they also allow end users to capture pictures or sounds on the job so that they can consult with colleagues or experts.

Tablet computer
(Courtesy Pogo Technology
Ltd., www.pogo-tech.com)

Tablet computers

These are basically laptops without the keyboard (or with a detachable keyboard). They are very useful for performance support and data entry on the job. The user draws on the screen itself or uses a stylus to tap on menu items. They can be strapped onto vehicles such as a truck dashboard or forklift truck or carried around a construction site or storeroom.

PERSISTENT COMPUTING VS. SYNCHRONIZING DATA

All of the mobile devices mentioned above can download data from the Internet or from another computer through a process that's generally called *synchronization* (or *sync* for short). The syncing process allows you to decide manually what gets transferred among devices or for the system to copy the latest edition of a file to all machines automatically. This means that you may work on a memo on your lap-

*PDA cell phone
(Courtesy Handspring)*

Smart cell phones and pagers

Forget about just talking into your phone; now you can type into it. "Smart" cell phones, widespread in Europe, are becoming more popular in other parts of the world; they allow you to browse wirelessly through miniature versions of Web sites, type short messages to other users, or receive automatic notifications of information such as flight delays or stock prices.

*Photo of Magellan GPS
system
(Courtesy Handspring)*

GPS

Global positioning devices use a system of satellites to pinpoint your location (down to a couple of feet) using a small device that periodically sends out signals. These are used, naturally, for locating yourself on a map and creating routes to a destination. Companies with a mobile workforce use these to track performance and as security devices to locate employees who may need help.

*Wearable computer
(Courtesy Casio)*

Wearable devices

Remember Dick Tracy? Futurists say we will soon be wearing wristwatches that are cell phones and Web browsers, earrings that play music, and necklaces that carry our ID and medical information.

top, then go to lunch, and use your PDA to add to your to-do list and enter contact data for the new client you just met. When you synchronize your devices, the memo from your laptop replaces the older copy of that memo on your PDA, but the new contact information and updated to-do list on your PDA are transferred to your laptop. In between sync sessions, your PDA is not connected to anything and therefore is not updated.

Another way to update information in a mobile device is through wireless connectivity. This means that by using a cellular modem or infrared local area network, your mobile device is always connected: It can access Web pages, send and receive e-mail, and perhaps receive cellular calls without being tethered to a phone line or network connection wire. The vision of having a device that is always on is sometimes called *persistent computing*. Cellular modems can use current cellular networks to send and receive data, but this can be a slow process. There will soon be new cellular standards, called third-generation (3G) systems, that will carry higher-speed data and voice capability. Obviously, the cellular approach can work in any area with cellular coverage, but sometimes this can be difficult within buildings. Within a building or room, wireless local area networks allow people to roam about with laptops or other pocket computing devices and send and receive data without wires using infrared connections. Some offices and colleges use this so that people can be in classrooms, offices, or meetings and be connected without having to plug into the network.

A final way that mobile devices can send or receive data is infrared "beaming" among the devices themselves. For example, Palm computers can "beam" users' electronic business cards (short files with the person's name, e-mail address, address, and phone numbers) directly to another Palm device within a range of a few feet. Other files, such as pictures or documents or spreadsheets, can also be beamed to other compatible devices. See Figure 1.1 for a visual summary of connectivity options.

Right now, you could carry a briefcase full of devices to be able to read electronic books, manage your schedule and contacts, make cell phone calls, and listen to MP3 music. But these devices are merging, and there are already combination devices: cell phone add-ons to a PDA, an MP3 player built into a digital camera, and cell phones that can browse the Internet on their tiny screens.

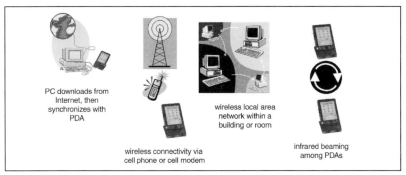

Figure 1.1 Wireless connectivity.

Envision this: You now have a delivery system for training, communication, collaboration, and performance aids that combines the following capabilities:

❏ Phone calls

❏ Music or audio playback

❏ Video and still-frame picture capture

❏ The ability to browse Web sites online

❏ E-mail send and receive

❏ Text and voice paging

❏ Global positioning and interactive map directions

❏ Multimedia, hypertext training, and documentation

❏ Expert systems and smart job aids

❏ Programs that monitor performance, take measurements, or perform calculations for workers

It's a pretty powerful bag of tricks.

HOW TO USE THIS BOOK

This book is designed to give you both the inspiration and the information you need to decide if mobile technologies make sense for your learning and performance needs. Chapters 2 through 8 each focus on a specific type of mobile device and contain these parts:

❑ A description of the technology in lay terms, including its common uses

❑ Applications of the technology for corporate training and performance improvement

❑ Case studies of actual or potential training and performance improvement solutions in various business settings

❑ An outline of how to create and distribute solutions using this device

❑ A checklist of do's and don'ts when considering the technology

❑ Resources for hardware, software, and solution providers

With this format, you can either concentrate on one particular technology such as pocket computers, or you can read about training and performance applications for all of these devices. If you already are familiar with the devices, you may want to concentrate on the case studies and instructions for applying them to learning and performance.

The final chapter, "Getting Up to Internet Speed," explores the kinds of changes that these new mobile technologies will bring to the design and management processes for corporate training. It explains why new instructional design and project management systems are needed, how to get management buy-in, how to get started with mobile learning and integrate it with your existing infrastructure, and how to keep up with developments in this area.

Knowledge in Your Pocket

PDAs for Communicating Knowledge and Performance Support

BELL NEXXIA'S sales employees are now receiving some of their product training while they are on the road. This Canadian telephony and Internet broadband provider is using handheld computers to download specific courses on product knowledge. Sales reps can do this right before meeting with a customer, so that they can be prepared with specific technical data and know how to position the product to the client. According to the company, this type of quick information gathering will be crucial to its business processes. Applications like this are the tip of the iceberg when it comes to the use of personal digital assistants (PDAs) for training and performance support.

WHAT ARE PDAs? EXAMPLES AND COMMON USES

PDAs are wallet-sized computers that were designed as basically digital calendar and address books. The best-known of these are generically known as Palm computers, although "Palm" is a registered trademark of Palm, Incorporated. Millions of these devices have been sold, first primarily to corporate executives who wanted a sleek and efficient way to track their busy schedules and take notes. These devices have a touch-sensitive display, and you get data into them in two ways: using buttons or stylus to make selections or write on the screen itself or download-ing information into them from a personal computer by cable or infrared beam.

There are two major standards for PDAs: the Palm oper-ating system and Microsoft Pocket PC operating system. These devices all look similar: they are about 4 inches high by 3 inches wide and less than 1 inch thick. They have either monochrome or color screens that can display buttons or text that you can select by tapping on them with a stylus, an area of the screen in which you can write with a stylus, and some physical buttons and dials. A number of vendors man-ufacture and sell devices based on these two standards. Although their functions and appearance are essentially the same, let's compare these two standards in the following chart:

Handheld Devices	**Pocket PCs**
Operating system	Palm OS	Microsoft Windows Pocket PC (also known as Windows CE and Pocket PC 2002)
Popular models	Palm, Handspring Visor, Sony Clié	Compaq iPAQ, Casio Cassiopia, HP Jornada
Popularity	These have about 70 percent of the market, especially in corporate applications; the Palm Pilot has been the standard among PDAs	Gaining in popularity because of their richer set of features and new models
Built-in applications	Address/phone book, calendar, to-do list, memo list, calculator	Stripped-down version of Microsoft Office (Pocket Word, Pocket Excel, Internet Explorer for the Pocket PC, Outlook, e-mail), Calendar, Contacts, Tasks, Reader (software to display E-books), and Notes
Data entry	By tapping buttons or writing with a stylus using a simplified writing style called Graffiti, downloading data from a personal computer, or attaching a small fold-up keyboard	By tapping buttons or writing with a stylus in natural handwriting on the screen, downloading data from a personal computer, or attaching a small fold-up keyboard
Ability to access Web sites	Must download Web viewer and only able to view "clipped" Web sites	Can display any Web site (although the screen is tiny)
Screen resolution	160 x 160 resolution; most have monochrome displays, but newer and more expensive models have 8-bit color displays with 256 colors	320 x 240 resolution 16-bit active matrix display with 65,000 colors
Audio and video display	Must purchase extra hardware module and software to play back audio and video	Built-in MP3 and Windows Media Player
Price	$100–350	$350–500

Another operating system and hardware standard is Symbian OS, the most popular models being made by Psion. These devices are fairly popular in Europe but do not have the user base in North America that the Palm and Pocket Windows systems enjoy.

Typically, PDAs come with some standard functions built into the read-only memory (see Figure 2.1):

- ❑ An address book
- ❑ A calendar
- ❑ A notepad or mini–word processor
- ❑ A to-do list
- ❑ A calculator
- ❑ An e-mail and Web browsing function

Figure 2.1 Typical PDA functions.

You can buy additional software that can be downloaded into the PDA by first installing it on a personal computer and then downloading it into the PDA by its sync function (also called "HotSync"). To sync data, you generally place the PDA in a cradle (see Figure 2.2) or connect it to a computer by a cable, or send files between the computer and

PDA by infrared ports on each device. When you sync data, the most current files from each computer get written to the other. For example if you enter a new address in your desktop computer in the morning, change the time of an appointment on your PDA and write a to-do note during lunch, and then sync the devices in the afternoon, the new address will be sent from your computer to the PDA, and your appointment and to-do notes from your PDA will be sent to your desktop computer, all with the push of one button on the cradle. To install new software or files, you merely call up an Install function on your computer that will place files to be installed into a separate directory, and these will automatically be downloaded to the PDA at the next sync session.

Figure 2.2 A PDA in the sync cradle. (Courtesy Handspring)

Although PDAs were never designed as training devices, they are perfect for a variety of short training modules, as well as for use as performance management and support tools. You can run interactive training programs on them, use them to display job aids or manuals, browse the Web, and play back audio, still pictures, and, on some units, motion video.

As a training manager or developer, you can use them to capture audio, stills, or video during needs-analysis sessions or for later use within a course or manual. There is even a plug-in module for a PDA that allows you to store and show PowerPoint slides when attached to a computer projector.

PDAs in Training

There are several ways to use PDAs in training. At the simplest level, you can download text documents that learners can read as time permits. The documents can be viewed using PDA versions of word processors; there are also e-book software programs that display text either horizontally or vertically, can change the type font and size, and can even automatically scroll through the pages so users do not have to keep pressing a key to continue reading. At a more complex level, you can create interactive programs with hyperlinks and graphics or even sophisticated learner interactions.

For example, AdvanceWork International has created English-as-a-Foreign-Language courses for pocket PC computers. Each Professional English course consists of eight study units, each with three to four lessons, for a total of twenty-five to twenty-eight lessons per course. Each study unit teaches listening, speaking, conversation practice and role playing, grammar, vocabulary, and exercises with interactive activities presented on the pocket PC. To supplement the pocket PC instruction, each course also includes ten live telephone conversations with a native English-speaking instructor. In these, the student is able to put into application the material that has been learned using the pocket PC. Additional instruction is available asynchronously via e-mail.

Up Close

Interview with
Jessica B. Figueiredo, President,
Empowering Technologies, Hillside, New Jersey

A good example of training and productivity software for PDAs is Lead by Values, one of a series of handheld computer–based leadership courses by Empowering Technologies. The software helps users identify their guiding values, put values into action, and measure the impact of their leadership styles. The interactive program includes a personal journal and questions to provoke thought and for assessment. Empowering Technologies develops mobile learning applications for the Palm OS and Pocket PC OS. The organization is developing libraries of content in the areas of leadership, teaming, creativity, and sales for the consumer market and contracting with various corporate entities to convert existing proprietary content into handheld performance support applications and custom (proprietary) learning applications.

What got you started in using the mobile device or devices?
Our company was founded by instructional designers and technologists interested in exploiting emerging technologies for adult learning. We found a gap in "reaching the unreachable" decentralized workforce. This group is often unable to participate in traditional learning environments with instructor-led courses because of geography and lack of time. Combine this with strained bandwidth and minimal time dedicated to learning and performance improvement, and you have a vast number of learners unable to access training. The handheld device—Palm OS in particular—was the most intriguing because of the amount of support from the device manufacturer, as well as the development tools available to work within this operating system. Its open architecture platform makes it quick and easy to develop third-party content.

Explain how the application is used. Who are the users, and what is the setting? For the Leadership Series—Lead by Values, in particular [see Figure 2.3]—we have targeted professionals interested in empowering themselves and taking responsibility for their own professional development. For corporate performance support solutions and custom learning applications, the users and settings vary from client to client.

Figure 2.3 Sample shots from Lead by Values.

Explain exactly how the application is created and then used. What software or programming language is used, who is the team that created this, and how do users get it and manipulate it on their own device? The application begins with content being converted into a formal design document based on traditional instructional design principles (including behavioral objectives and criterion-referenced testing). The content is then storyboarded using a proprietary tool we have developed in-house, and the application is built using an offshoot of the BASIC programming language designed by NSBasic. The graphic user interface [GUI], text, graphics, navigation, and user interactions are hand-coded and tested.

The application can be deployed in several different ways: downloaded from a Web server and then HotSync'd, sent to a computer via e-mail and then HotSync'd, or by infrared beaming peer-to-peer between PDAs. A central database resides on the device; however, we also build data conduits to send data back to the desktop or Web server to be recorded in a central location and evaluated.

How long does it typically take to design and deploy such an application? One twenty-minute application can be designed, developed, and tested in four weeks. This time frame may vary depending on the complexities of the databases and conduits to be built.

What were the biggest challenges or unexpected hurdles? The biggest challenges were the small screen, no audio (for the Palm OS, although this is changing soon), and a lack of standardized platforms being supported in the corporate environment. The biggest hurdle was buy-in from corporate clients that this is a viable and complementary learning platform that enhances their existing e-learning infrastructure.

What advice would you give to fellow training, business performance, and communications professionals with regard to getting into the use of mobile devices? Start now! The tools and support are out there. The development environments are new but very stable and secure. Start with a small application. You'll find the rapid deployment and development increase return on investment versus expensive computer-based and Web-based training environments.

PDAs in Performance Support

PDAs are a perfect medium for delivering on-the-spot performance support, such as reference guides, repair manuals, product knowledge materials, and even small expert systems that solve problems. In addition, they can be used for personal performance enhancement by enabling users to enter data, such as budgets, project management information, and schedules.

Cisco has created a PDA-based guide for one of its products. The Catalyst 8540 MSR Modules/Adapters Guide is an interactive quick reference guide designed for use with pocket PC handheld devices (see Figure 2.4). To view it, users must first download and install the guide files from Cisco's Web site and must have Macromedia Flash Player for Pocket PC installed on their handheld system. The Pocket PC edition of the quick reference guide presents detailed information about interface modules and port adapters for the Catalyst 8540 MSR Multiservice Switch Router. Users can browse functional descriptions of the modules and port adapters, find which chassis slots accept them, identify connectors for the required cabling, and view animated illustration instructions.

Off-the-shelf productivity software includes applications like Taskmanager (see Figure 2.5), an application that helps users track and manage projects.

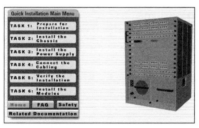

Figure 2.4 Cisco interactive Quick Guide for Pocket PCs.

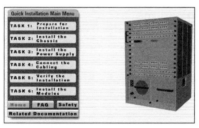

Figure 2.5 Taskmanager project management software from Pocketmanager (www.pocketmanager.com).

Up Close

Interview with
Chris Hopkins, developer of SCATA Logbook
for Performance Support at the
Royal College of Anaesthetists, London

Chris Hopkins is specialist registrar in anesthesia and joint author of the SCATA Logbook, a software tool for medical students. He is a member of the Society for Computers and Technology in Anaesthesia (SCATA), a fourteen-year-old U.K.-based medical society that provides a forum for discussion and demonstration of a wide range of issues related to computing and technology in and around anesthesia. The SCATA Anaesthetic Logbook for the Symbian Platform was written by Chris Hopkins, Alastair Lack, and Jim Watt on behalf of SCATA, whose Web site is *www.scata.org.uk.*

Briefly describe what mobile device you are using and what the applications consist of. The Royal College of Anaesthetists in the United Kingdom recommends that all trainees keep a permanent record of anesthetics given, in the form of a logbook that can be presented at regular intervals to their supervising physicians. Modern handheld devices are ideally suited to collect this information and present it in the desired format. We have designed a logbook for Symbian-based handhelds such as the Psion Revo, Series 5mx, and Series 7.

What got you started in using the mobile device or devices? I became interested in using mobile devices in medicine when I was a new doctor on the ward and trying to keep track of an ever-changing list of patients. The Psion 3a database proved an invaluable means of recording the information. Gaining confidence, I soon turned my attention to the built-in programming tools and rapidly learned how to write short applications to help automate my work on the ward. By the time I started in anesthetics, I had built up a good basic knowledge of OPL. When I was presented with a paper-based logbook, I quickly set about making an electronic version, which I realized would be a far more efficient way to collate all the information for my tutors. With the release of the Psion Series 5, I set about adapting my logbook to suit the new operating system, and when I finished, I posted the program on the Web as freeware. Despite the presence of other anesthetic logbooks, my software became popular among trainees in the United Kingdom, and with the release of the Psion Revo, SCATA approached me to help write a new version of its logbook that would better suit the current range of EPOC handhelds.

Explain how the application is used. Who are the users, and what is the setting? The logbook is used predominantly by trainees in anesthesia in the hospital setting to record the number and nature of cases attended, allowing an assessment to be made of the level of experience an individual has achieved. Standardized reports can be generated and presented at their regular assessments.

What have been the business or productivity results? The program is distributed as freeware by SCATA. Although we designed the application for the United Kingdom, its customizability and ease of use have found it a worldwide market.

Explain exactly how the application is created and then used. What software or programming language is used, who is the team that created this, and how do users get it and manipulate it on their device? The application was created using OPL, a rapid application development language that has been distributed along with Psion-based handheld machines since 1984. It is a procedural-based language, very similar to BASIC, that allows the development of applications on the device itself, which has produced a large, loyal user base. The operating system is written in C++, which many users prefer to OPL, but the majority of EPOC freeware and shareware has been written in OPL. The logbook was developed by a team of three doctors with an interest in handheld devices and is distributed as a free download from the SCATA Web site in a self-installing format. The program can be installed via a desktop machine or simply on the device itself.

The basic logbook screen shot [see Figure 2.6] shows its general look and feel. Users input data with the keyboard and touch screen. Information entered can be displayed in a customizable, scrolling list view [see Figure 2.7]. Reports can be generated and displayed on screen, printed, or exported to other applications such as spreadsheets.

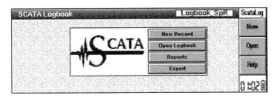

Figure 2.6 SCATALOG medical job aid.

How long does it typically take to design and deploy such an application? The logbook took seven months to develop to a level that could be released as a Beta version because all the work had to be completed in our spare time.

What were the biggest challenges or unexpected hurdles? The largest challenge was to produce an application that was flexible enough so that users can customize it to meet their particular needs.

What are your future plans for mobile device applications for training or business communications with your employees, students, or customers? I plan to continue to develop mobile applications because of the ever-increasing number of handheld devices that trainees carry. I intend to focus more on an educational program for my next project.

What advice would you give to fellow training, business performance, and communications professionals with regard to getting into the use of mobile devices? There is a large number of dedicated programmers with many years of experience who are willing to help and give advice and who contribute regularly to the various user groups. Software development kits are also available to download from Symbian, which is behind the operating system used by Psion.

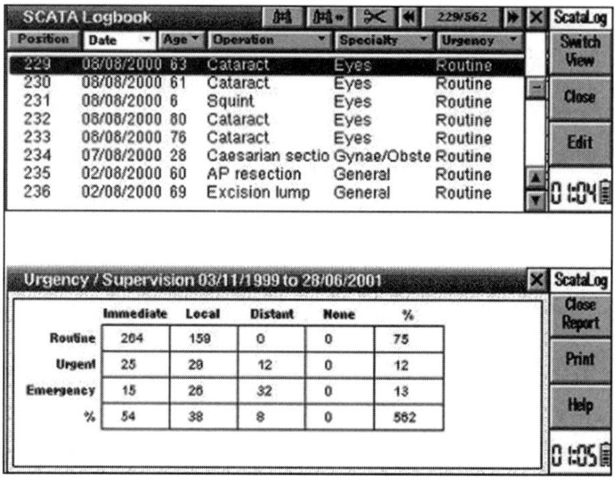

SCATA Logbook   229/562   ScataLog   Switch View   Close   Edit

Position	Date	Age	Operation	Specialty	Urgency
229	08/08/2000	63	Cataract	Eyes	Routine
230	08/08/2000	61	Cataract	Eyes	Routine
231	08/08/2000	6	Squint	Eyes	Routine
232	08/08/2000	80	Cataract	Eyes	Routine
233	08/08/2000	76	Cataract	Eyes	Routine
234	07/08/2000	28	Caesarian sectio	Gynae/Obste	Routine
235	02/08/2000	60	AP resection	General	Routine
236	02/08/2000	69	Excision lump	General	Routine

Urgency / Supervision 03/11/1999 to 28/06/2001   ScataLog   Close Report   Print   Help

	Immediate	Local	Distant	None	%
Routine	264	159	0	0	75
Urgent	25	29	12	0	12
Emergency	15	26	32	0	13
%	54	38	8	0	562

Figure 2.7 Screen shots from the SCATALOG.

PDAs for Designing and Managing Training

PDAs can be used for managing the training function also. There are a number of shareware or inexpensive programs for designing and managing classroom courses, and although most are designed for schoolteachers rather than corporate trainers, they can be quite useful. For example, ThoughtManager for Teachers (see Figure 2.8) is a powerful outliner tool and educational database that allows teachers to create and organize the hundreds of ideas, lessons, tasks, problems, solutions, and assessment data that good teaching requires. It has over seventy-five downloadable educational resource outlines and templates for easy reference, including many kinds of lesson plan templates. This is a terrific resource for a train-the-trainer session, especially when the goal is to help people become better "occasional" trainers doing coaching and cross-training in the workplace.

Figure 2.8 ThoughtManager for Teachers.

DO IT YOURSELF: BUYING AND CREATING PDA APPLICATIONS

There are several ways to use PDAs in learning and performance. The simplest is to use the built-in tools like the address book and calendar feature to help others (and yourself) manage time and tasks better. More powerful and targeted applications will require you to buy or create more specific programs. The good thing about either of these options is that they are generally inexpensive and easy.

OFF-THE-SHELF SOFTWARE

There are thousands of PDA programs available, and many are free or under $30 for a single-user license. Most of the downloadable programs like this are more in the category of job aids than actual training materials, but some combine both.

One example of a free teaching and performance-improvement tool for medical education is the Handango Medical Student Suite, a set of small programs for the Palm OS that includes a huge medical reference database with medical terms; a medical calculator that calculates commonly used but cumbersome formulas like body mass index and

temperature conversions; and textbook information on topics such as types of wounds, sutures, needles, and surgical
knots. As PDAs become more popular, we can expect to see
more vendors creating applications for them, such as Lead
by Values. Finally, there is a growing library of e-books that
can be displayed on a Pocket PC or Palm computer; these
are specially formatted books that display well on a small
screen and are readable using a special viewer that can be
downloaded separately.

When you are licensing off-the-shelf software, remember
to check on specifications and compatibility:

❑ The operating system used (Palm, Pocket PC, or Symbian)

❑ What manufacturer and models are compatible

❑ The amount of memory needed to install and run the
application

❑ What operating system the desktop software needs to be
loaded on in order to sync to the PDA (Windows, Mac OS,
Linux)

❑ If any add-on modules are included or needed (such as
extra memory cards or an audio player)

CREATING YOUR OWN APPLICATIONS

The process of developing PDA applications runs the gamut
from complete simplicity (creating a simple document on
your word processor) to extreme complexity (actually creating programs in a programming language). Basically, there
are two ways to do it.

The first way is to create a document or file that can be
displayed using another PDA application. For example, you
can create a text file in Microsoft Word, or a spreadsheet in
Excel, or a Web site in an html authoring tool such as
Netscape Composer or Dreamweaver. These files are created

on your desktop or laptop computer and then transferred to PDAs using the sync function. They are viewed on the PDA using either built-in software (on Pocket PCs, the Pocket Word or Internet Explorer) or third-party viewers (on Palm OS units, Word document viewers like QuickOffice, CspotRun (see Figure 2.9), or Web site viewers such as AvantGo).

Figure 2.9 A text document displayed using the CSpotRun reader available at http://32768.com/cspotrun/.

Another possibility is to use a program like Adobe Acrobat to save a document in a standard format that preserves layout, fonts, and graphics as they are viewed using either its free viewer on the Web or its free viewer for the Palm OS. Once a document is saved as a .pdf (portable document format) file using Acrobat, you can simply transfer it to your Palm computer using built-in menus, as illustrated in Figure 2.10.

The second way to develop your own application is by using an authoring tool like Macromedia Flash or a programming language to create a more interactive and customized-looking application (the Cisco application in Figure 2.4 is an example). There are versions of BASIC and other programming languages designed for the Palm OS (see the previous example of Lead by Values). These are created on a desktop PC, and then the code is transferred to the PDA. This requires much more expertise, but the applications can be much more sophisticated than simple documents or Web pages with embedded links and graphics.

Figure 2.10 Transferring a .pdf file to your Palm computer.

◻ CHECKLIST FOR EVALUATION AND LAUNCH OF PDAS

◻ If there are PDAs already in use in your organization, what is the standard in terms of operating system and model? If there is a large installed base, design your applications around it.

❏ If there is not an installed base of PDAs for your target users, choose among the models available:

  ❏ Palm OS models are cheaper and have more off-the-shelf software available for them.

  ❏ Pocket PC models are more expensive but have better resolution and built-in mini-versions of familiar Microsoft Office applications.

  ❏ Other devices that do not use the previous two common operating systems may be good for your application but may have less long-term support in the marketplace. Such devices include proprietary e-book viewers that are primarily designed to read text, but may have some organizer or audio player functions built in. But beware of buying a system that may soon be orphaned.

❏ Find one or two compelling but small applications for PDAs, and quickly create and try out prototypes with a limited audience of opinion leaders in your organization.

❏ Decide on no more than three standard applications for creating and viewing your applications. For example, decide that you will use Word and QuickOffice for manuals or Flash for animated instruction.

❏ Create a roll-out for users that includes training on how to use the PDA and your applications, as well as how to download other useful applications from the Web. Make sure users know how to back up and sync files.

❏ Build a support infrastructure, including help files on the Web and in print, a help desk, and replacement units.

❏ Create a way for users to share tips and applications that they create themselves; this can be through an e-mail group or a Web site on your intranet.

RESOURCES

As PDAs are becoming more popular, many organizations are creating software for both the Palm OS and Pocket PC operating systems. These programs can be purchased in stores and through catalogs, but the largest selection is online. Following are some of the best sites for finding these applications:

www.palmgear.com, featuring links to Palm OS software and hardware

www.microsoft.com/mobile/default.asp, the Microsoft Pocket PC site

www.pdaED.com, dedicated to PDAs in education

www.pocketmanager.com, for pocket books and management productivity software

For specialized applications in vertical industries, check out the following Web sites:

www.pdaMD.com, PDA applications in medicine

www.pdaJD.com, PDAs in law

www.pdaRE.com, PDAs in real estate

www.pdaFN.com, PDAs in finance

3

More Than Napster

Using Digital Audio for Corporate News and Training

AUDIO **IS** a much-overlooked technology for delivering information; in today's mobile environment, it can be a very effective solution. A few decades ago, audio was a popular medium for providing training tips and for corporate news. I remember being asked to help improve the training and communication for a client whose field representatives called on farmers to sell bovine genetics—artificial insemination for cattle. The technicians worked almost entirely on the road. It was expensive and inconvenient to bring them to a central location for training, and they were already overloaded with print materials. We designed a radio news format series that was distributed on audiocassettes so that they could listen to an interesting mix of interviews, tips from colleagues, training refreshers, and corporate news while they were driving.

Audiocassettes are far from being a new technology, but the need still exists to provide road-bound employees—whether they are driving on sales calls, commuting in the car, or traveling by plane or train—with valuable information in what might otherwise be rather unproductive time.

WHAT IS DIGITAL AUDIO?

Audio from traditional sources like microphones, audiotapes (that you buy or produce yourself), records, or CDs can be digitized and played back on pocket computers or portable audio devices. You have undoubtedly heard of MP3, one format for storing digital audio and made famous by Napster, the Web site where people shared mostly illegal copies of their CD collections online. MP3 and other similar technologies allow you to download or create digital audio and then create "jukeboxes" where your files (individual songs, interviews, or training audio clips) can be displayed, organized, and downloaded into a tiny portable player.

We typically see digital audio files played back on tiny portable devices like the Rio 800, pictured in Figure 3.1. They can also be played on desktop computers or PDAs that have playback software installed and even on some cell phones. You can purchase inexpensive adapters that allow you to play back audio from a small MP3 player using any audiocassette deck, for example, on a home or car stereo (see Figure 3.2). The Sony Clié handheld device comes with an MP3 player and headphones as standard features (see Figure 3.3). Finally, there are other digital audio devices that are designed specifically for museums and play audio descriptions of exhibits as the visitors approach them.

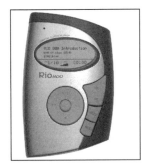

Figure 3.1 Rio 800 MP3 player. (Courtesy Rio Audio, a division of SONICblue)

Figure 3.2 You can listen to files from your MP3 player on a cassette deck using an adapter like this. (Photo courtesy Rio Audio, a division of SONICblue)

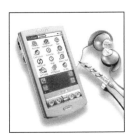

Figure 3.3 Sony Clié handheld PEG-N710C with MP3 player built in. (Courtesy Sony Electronics, Inc.)

You can use digital audio devices in a number of ways— for example:

- ❏ Provide corporate news in a radio show format.
- ❏ Set up audio tours of your facility for visitors or new employees.
- ❏ Deploy audio job aids that can be used even if workers are using their hands.
- ❏ Set up a mechanism to allow trainees to buy audio books on various business topics.
- ❏ Record, archive, and distribute executive speeches for stockholders, employees, and the general public.

TECHNOLOGICAL DETAILS

MP3 is probably the digital audio format that you have heard most about lately (the acronym stands for Moving Picture Experts Group, which is the industry organization that approved the standard in 1992). But it is one of several popular formats, and so it is important to know about the range of options available. The standards that are used to digitize and play back audio are called *codecs* (for encode and decode).

The first popular standard digital audio format was the WAV format, which was the standard file format for audio built into Windows 95. Many audio tracks that are used in CD-ROM training programs use this format. Although you can create and play back WAV files on any Windows computer using just the audio accessories built into Windows, the sizes are a bit large for storage on anything but a hard drive or CD-ROM.

The MP3 standard for digitizing and storing audio files provides for high-quality reproduction with smaller files than from previous formats like the WAV standard. For example, an hour of music encoded in the WAV format requires about 600 megabytes of memory to achieve CD quality, while an hour's worth of music stored in the MP3 format requires only 32 megabytes of storage. Ogg Vorbis is a royalty-free compressed audio format that is very much like MP3; its file extension is OGG.

Two of the first widely circulated consumer MP3 tools were Winamp and MacAmp, but probably the most widely known application is RealJukebox from RealNetworks. RealJukebox lets users "rip" CDs, which means they can insert an audio CD into their computer CD player and digitize the whole CD or just parts of it and store and organize the files on a hard drive. Once organized into a "jukebox" on a hard drive, the files can be downloaded into a portable player like a Rio by means of a serial or USB cable (both serial and USB connectors have become standard on laptop and desktop computers).

A more recent introduction from Microsoft is the WMA (Windows Media Audio) format, which allows you to store files half the size of MP3s. Although most of the early digital audio players supported only MP3 files, many of the recent players also support WMA, as do all of the PDAs that use the Pocket PC format.

MIDI (musical instrument digital interface) files are digital files used specifically for music. This format is used to record files from a synthesizer or to play back files on a computer or through a synthesizer.

MP3 and WMA are the most common formats for digital music, but there is another type of format, called *streaming audio,* that is found on the Internet. *Streaming* means that you do not have to wait for an entire file to download from the Internet before you can play it; rather, it downloads as it plays, which makes large files available more quickly to the user. However, streaming files generally cannot be saved to a user's hard drive. The most popular streaming audio format is RealAudio, a proprietary format of RealNetworks. If you want to create RealAudio files, you must license the creation software from RealNetworks, but the playback software can be freely downloaded from the Web site.

Some of the other formats you may encounter are ATRAC3 from Sony, LQT from Liquid Audio, and Audible.com's format for audio books that can compress spoken word files to very tiny sizes. These file formats build in protection schemes for copyrighted works.

Now that you know a something about the technical side of things, let's explore applications.

AUDIO BOOKS AND TRAINING CLIPS

You are probably familiar with books on tape; many commuters and people taking long car trips buy or rent these to catch up on their favorite author or check out some self-help topics. Although these are still a viable medium, the realm of digital audio has made more topics available and has made it easier to find and distribute these solutions.

If you are responsible for functions like management or sales training, you will find many excellent generic training sources available online. These will not replace a course and actual practice in most cases, but they are a useful adjunct to traditional training sessions and are especially useful for continuing executive education. Unlike administering a library of training books where you spend your time shelving and tracking down books, you can create accounts with some online purveyors of audio books and training courses, and trainees can download what they like. You might send out customized e-mail messages or create a Web site that includes direct links to these sources to encourage employees to take advantage of them.

Audible.com is one of the Internet's leading sources of digital spoken word audio from the world's leading publishers (see Figure 3.4). Well over 18,000 titles are available for purchase, download, and playback, including best-selling audio books, audio versions of major newspapers, and specialized audio programs. Programs available from Audible.com can be played back on PCs and laptops, and through a variety of mobile devices, such as MP3 players, Pocket PCs, Handspring PDAs, and cell phones.

Figure 3.4 An example of Audible.com's business titles.

Any corporation or institution can take advantage of Audible's Audio Integration Services to convey audio versions of research, news, strategy, and sector updates to mobile employees and clients. You can create your own mobile audio "channel," which can feature audio programs specific to your audience, as well as offer targeted branded news and business content, like the *Wall Street Journal* and the *New York Times*.

Audible offers a number of services—for example:

❐ Editorial oversight and production of custom audio programming

❐ Delivery of content through existing financial institution internal and client Web sites

❐ Conversion of existing audio to digital, downloadable, and telematic delivery formats

❐ Online storage and delivery (hosting) of secure, copyright-protected audio content

❐ Group-specific special offers and discounts for premium audio content, such as best-selling audio books and audio versions of leading newspapers

❐ Usage and delivery tracking and reporting

❐ Billing and transaction management

❐ Technical support for software and audio devices

Another source for digital audio files is Real.com, which offers free audio and video news from sources like Bloomberg and the *Financial Times*. RealNetworks now offers a service that allows users to play back audio news on cell phones.

An increasing number of Web sites offer digital audio "lecturettes" that can be downloaded for free. For example, the PowerPointers Web site features short pointers from expert speakers that help presenters build, plan, and deliver better speeches and sales presentations (see Figure 3.5).

Figure 3.5 Free audio courses on topics like presentation skills are available online. (Courtesy of PowerPointers.com, Because Great Presentations Are What You Need To Succeed)

Up Close

Interview with
Nancy Proctor, Business Development Manager,
Antenna Audio, London

Antenna Audio is a leading developer of audio tour technologies with offices throughout Europe and North America. Its diverse and well-known clients include the Art Institute of Chicago, the Vatican Museum, the Louvre, the Hong Kong Tourist Association, the National Zoo in Washington, D.C., Graceland (the Elvis Presley homestead), and Royal Hawaiian Cruises. Its portable audio players, which museum goers can rent in museums, provide information about exhibits.

With your extensive background in doing technology for interpretive audio tours, what are some of the newer technologies you are exploring? With the rise of digital media and the arrival of high-speed Internet connections, a wide range of opportunities has arisen for museums to reach out to new audiences. Audio is now a completely fluid medium, capable of being distributed in digital form across a wide variety of platforms. Antenna Audio's mission has always been to provide educational access and income opportunities for our museum partners. Now it is possible to project this mission beyond the walls of the museum.

Antenna Audio is pursuing a number of initiatives.

For some time, visitors to attractions have been able to purchase audiocassettes and compact disks of the audio tour as a souvenir and educational tool. Now, Antenna Audio's Web audio tour service enables visitors to preview the audio tour of an attraction online and even download the tour to their personal MP3 players. Antenna Audio won the TiLE 2001 exhibition's Best New Product or Service award for this development of online audio tours.

Now audiences can take the Web with them wherever they go—on their personal organizers, pocket PCs, and Internet phones. Antenna Audio redevelops fixed Web sites into "PDA portals," providing audiences with the information they need about organizations while on the move. Antenna Audio has an exclusive agreement with AvantGo (*http://avantgo.com/channels/*) to make museums' PDA portals available as AvantGo "channels," so that mobile users around the world can receive their favorite museums' information along with daily news and mobile entertainment on their handheld computers, Internet phones, and PDAs.

Antenna Audio can now combine its audio tours of exhibitions and collections with visual walk-throughs to create a fully audiovisual three-dimensional space that virtual visitors can stroll through with the same freedom as they move through the actual gallery. Antenna Audio's "real virtual tours" present artworks and objects in the gallery without distortion or pixelation, welcoming close study and giving the most faithful representation of the actual exhibition possible. Antenna Audio virtual tours can link each object in the gallery to further information, including text, audio clips, video footage, and more images. As a result, the actual gallery space becomes the organizing and navigational structure for a whole wealth of museum information, just as it is in the real world. The Antenna Audio virtual tour can bring the entire institution, including its archives and museum shop, into one media-rich electronic catalog that can be distributed via the Web, CD-ROM, or DVD to desktop computers, handheld devices, and e-book readers.

Antenna Audio's multimedia tours are designed to take advantage of the latest developments in handheld computer technology to provide a complete audiovisual experience of visitor attractions. Using pocket PCs, Antenna Audio can stream audio, video, and still images to visitors according to their location on site and their personal profiles, including language, age, and interests. These multimedia tours allow museums and visitor attractions to display digital images of related art works and information that cannot be physically included in the exhibition. Video interviews with artists and experts, data sheets, drawings, and statistical information that is too cumbersome to display as wall texts can be included in the show. Through a database-driven content delivery system, the museum also has the ability to interact with its visitors throughout the multimedia tour, collecting information on the visitor's movements and interests in the museum and suggesting related displays, experiences, questions, or activities for the visitor to try. The entire tour is fully audio enabled, to ensure a complete sensory experience and the highest-quality interpretation.

Antenna Audio's X-plorer MP3 player now permits visitor attractions to interact with visitors through their audio tour in order to find out more about them or provide interactive learning opportunities alongside the tour [see Figure 3.6]. The X-plorer can be programmed to ask visitors questions and record their responses in a variety of sophisticated multiple-choice formats. Questions and quizzes can be built into the audio tour of a museum or visitor attraction to create a fully interactive experience for visits. Visitor responses can then be downloaded from the X-plorer and analyzed through customized statistic interfaces, offering teachers, for example, the means of recording and analyzing their students' activities on the learning tour of the museum. Antenna Audio won the TiLE 2001 exhibition's Best New Innovation award for this application.

Figure 3.6 Interactive audio tour device.

Cultural tourism is the major reason behind most travel decisions. The desire to see and learn has tremendous impact on hotel, restaurant, and airline expenditures. In a sense, these are parasitic enterprises that feed off the cultural institutions that are the main attraction. For the past couple of years, Antenna has been considering ways in which we can position our partner institutions so that a portion of this income flows directly back to the museums and heritage sites with which we work.

Antenna Audio is in a unique position in that we link most of the world's major cultural institutions through our network of audio tours. Antenna Audio is working with AMICO, the Art Museum Image Consortium [www.amigo.org], to support efforts to make audiovisual content of a cultural nature available via the Web and other digital platforms. Syndicating our combined content, we can supply comprehensive audio and visual information on cultural tourism to various sellers and information providers—for example, Internet travel sites, airlines, hotels, and distance-learning sites.

CORPORATE NEWS SHOWS AND EXECUTIVE COMMUNICATION

As digital technologies are blurring the lines between public relations, employee communications, and training, new opportunities for providing news to internal and external audiences are emerging. Based on formats like audio interviews and radio news shows, MP3 formats are being used to keep employees and investors aware of important events, provide coaching, and broadcast messages to field staff.

UP CLOSE

Interview with
Ralph Schmitt, Executive Vice President,
Cypress Semiconductor, San Jose, California

Cypress has created some of the world's leading semiconductor products, with over 4,400 employers worldwide.

Please describe your application of mobile devices. Briefly describe what device you are using and what the applications consist of. We use MP3 players to broadcast company messages to our sales and marketing departments. We began using the players because we were experiencing frustration with communications to the far ends of the world.

Explain how the application is used and created. Salespeople download the MP3 files to their company-deployed players and listen to key messages [see Figure 3.7]. The application is done in conjunction with Rioport, a company that takes our recorded messages and translates them into the proper format. It takes only a few hours to deploy these messages.

What have been the business or productivity results, and what are your plans? We've achieved fast communication and consistency in messages. We will migrate to a Palm or RIM (Research in Motion) pager device to push product data and availability wirelessly.

What were the biggest challenges or unexpected hurdles? Ensuring all download messages to players are foolproof and simple.

What advice would you give to fellow training, business performance, and communications professionals with regard to getting into the use of mobile devices? Shut off all other ways of communicating.

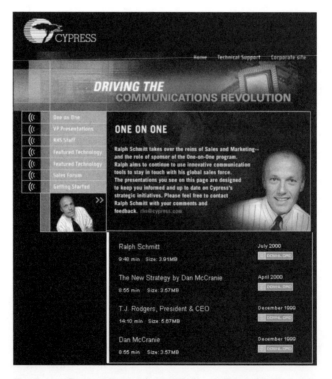

Figure 3.7 Cypress Semiconductor Employee Communications uses MP3 downloads. (Courtesy Cypress Semiconductor)

How to Create and Distribute Digital Audio Files

It is relatively easy to create and distribute digital audio files—and even easier to find sources where your trainees can download their own. It may be simplest to start by using some of the Internet sites that offer audio books and speeches, like Audible.com. You can set up an account and fill out user preferences that will enable Audible to send you e-mail updates when there are new products on your topics of interest. You can do this yourself and encourage end users to do this on their own. The next step from here is to contract with a company like Audible to create your own "channel" that includes products relevant to your company's industry or typical training topics, as well as content that you create yourself (see Figure 3.8).

Figure 3.8 Customizing Audible.com for your interests and hardware.

You will probably soon run into situations where you want to create your own content, a process that is quite easy. Any computer running a current version of Windows has a built-in sound recorder that you will find under Accessories when you click on the Start button. If you plug a microphone into your computer (almost every computer today has a sound card with a mike input), you can use this simple software to record by pressing the red Record button on the panel, which will save the audio into a WAV file format. You can distribute WAV files by e-mail or create your own "jukebox" on a Web site that has links where your end users can click to download the file.

Remember that WAV files are quite large and cannot be played back on the new digital music devices, so you will probably want to convert files to an MP3 format or create them in this format to start. There are many software tools that will allow you to do this, including the very popular dBpowerAMP Music Converter, which is free to download at *http://admin.dbpoweramp.com/*. As you can see in Figure 3.9, the process is easy. You can configure dBpowerAMP to come up automatically whenever you right-click on an audio file in Windows Explorer. Or you can start up the program and choose the file you want to convert. It allows you to convert among several popular file formats, and you can choose the rate of compression (smaller files have worse quality) and where you want to save the file.

You probably will want to create files that are more complex than just something you record into a microphone. Usually, the audio files are edited to eliminate glitches and to mix in music or sound effects. To do this, you can buy a digital audio mixer, which is a device into which you can plug various devices, like a CD player, tape player, and microphone. You can use dials and levers to adjust the rela-

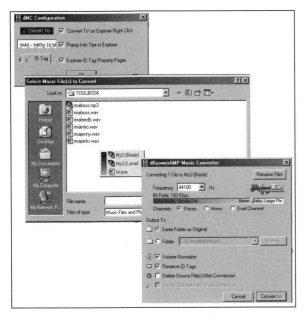

Figure 3.9 Converting an audio file from WAV to MP3 using dBpowerAMP from Illustrate (http://admin.dbpoweram.com/).

tive levels of these devices and then save the output as a digital file.

You can also record one source at a time directly into your PC and mix the files later using digital mixing software like Cool Edit Pro from Syntrillium Software (see Figure 3.10). Although professional versions of digital audio mixers may cost several hundred dollars, there are plenty of free or demo versions that will do the work in many cases. Software like this allows you to blend a number of files over each other (like an audio track under a narrator) and to cut and paste segments of digital audio files just like word processing, by showing you graphic representations of a time line and your various audio clips.

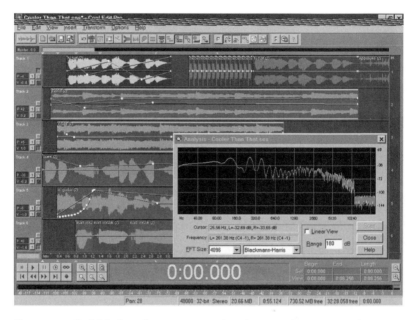

Figure 3.10 Cool Edit Pro allows you to record and mix together various audio sources. (Courtesy Syntrillium Software)

To record from an audiotape or record, connect the device to your line-in jack on your computer's sound card using a cable with a stereo RCA-to-headphone cable. This has two plugs on one end that you plug into the left and right output jacks on the audio player or amplifier and a smaller jack that you plug into the line-in jack on the computer. Start up your digital audio software and specify the recording source. Generally you can select whether you want to record from the built-in CD player, the line-in source, or mic-in for a microphone. You will also need to specify the output format (MP3, WAV, or something else).

Most digital audio software has a screen that looks like a traditional tape recorder, with a red Record button as well as

Stop/Pause, Forward, and Rewind buttons. To record from your audio source, press the Record button and start playing back your source. You may have to adjust the level of the recording input using a volume control or slider, so you may need a few tries before you complete the actual recording. Most software allows you to specify the quality of the recording; 128 kilobytes per second is generally fine for most recordings. You can create a number of small digital files and then weave them together using the digital editing software.

There are a number of options with regard to distributing digital audio files. Perhaps the easiest is to attach them to an e-mail message. For example, you can set up a distribution list of people who have taken a particular course and send them refreshers by e-mail. When they receive the attachment, they can download it to their computers and listen there or download the files to their MP3 players.

Another option is to create your own "jukebox" on one or more intranet pages. You can model these pages on commercial sites like Audible.com or use a format like Cypress Semiconductor uses to post its executive interviews for employees, investors, and the press. Include instructions for users on how to download the files plus links to popular free digital music player software. Again, try out some of commercial sites to see how they do it. A more comprehensive solution would be to contract with a vendor like Audible.com that can create digital files for you and host your own customized site, including the kinds of news, books, and industry links that are relevant to your organization.

☐ CHECKLIST FOR LAUNCHING DIGITAL AUDIO

☐ What kinds of information might be communicated effectively by audio? Consider speeches, industry news, interviews, training refreshers, and sales tips.

☐ Who is your audience, and where are they likely to listen to the audio? Here are some interesting possibilities:

  ☐ If you have a highly mobile workforce, consider whether it would be willing to use their commuting time to listen to training or news. You can buy MP3 players and car cassette adapters or encourage people to listen on the bus or train.

  ☐ You might purchase a dozen or so small digital audio players and load them with popular management books or training tips, and distribute them for free in your corporate gym. Instead of listening to hip-hop music, your employees can improve their minds as well as their bodies.

  ☐ Distribute comfortable headphones so that people can listen to audio books or speeches at their desks or using their laptops on airplanes.

  ☐ Create self-guided training and tours using the systems popular in museums.

☐ Do you have the proper playback hardware? Many corporate desktop computers do not have sound cards (even when they come as a free part of a computer package, some information services departments remove them so that the noise will not be distracting to workers).

☐ Consider the bulk purchase of small digital audio players that can be given or loaned out through your training department, information technology department, or corporate library.

☐ If you buy MP3 players, find ones that support a large number of codecs, such as MP3, WMA, or Audible formats. The most flexible ones have upgradable firmware, which means that you can download new codecs into the device's read-only memory.

☐ Make sure that you publicize your audio distribution system, and keep it lively with fresh content.

RESOURCES

Now that digital music players are becoming common, we can expect to see more Web sites devoted to distributing not only music but various nonfiction book titles and training courses.

Following are some of the most comprehensive sources for digital audio content as well as software to create digital audio yourself:

www.audible.com, devoted to selling digital audio files, including many popular books, for reasonable prices

www.real.com, streaming audio site containing hundreds of music and news channels

www.zdnet.com, for tutorials, free or inexpensive downloadable software for playing and creating digital audio, plus reviews and comparisons of new digital players

Not for Spies Only

Digital Input and Output Devices

THERE IS a plethora of digital devices that will allow you to capture still and motion images, text, and audio; some of these are single-purpose devices and some are intriguing multifunction units. You undoubtedly know that media producers use digital cameras, scanners, and audio recorders to create training materials and documentation. What you may not realize is that these devices are so small, inexpensive, and easy to use that they can become part of the toolbox that trainers and business performance consultants can use in analyzing problems, documenting performance, and collaborating with colleagues. What's more, putting these devices in the hands of end users can help to store and manage collective knowledge and create instant visual communities of practice.

Along with input devices to capture and manipulate digital data, there are ways to use PDAs and cameras as digital output devices—kind of like a slide tray or video player in your pocket. Because there are so many different kinds of devices, we will cover them one by one, looking at the technology and how to use it, as well as some examples of how these devices are being employed.

DIGITAL AUDIO

In the previous chapter on digital audio, we discussed how to create audio files from your computer and then store and play them back using a variety of codecs (compression/decompression schemes) and audio players. Here we will describe some gizmos that allow you to create digital audio in the field.

Probably the most common type of digital recorder is a voice recorder, a device about the size of a small microphone that records onto solid-state built-in memory or to a removable media storage device, like a smart card. The Olympus model pictured in Figure 4.1 is a good example; it allows you to record up to twenty-two hours of material and then download it to a PC. Through the use of voice recognition technology, your recorded words can then be transformed into word processed text with quite a high degree of reliability given a clean recording. Many recorders like this one also allow you to download files into them, such as MP3 music files or speech files, so they can be used as a portable player.

Many of these players have selectable recording formats, so that you can choose lower-quality but longer recording time, or higher-quality (which is better for speech-to-text translation) but shorter recording time.

Figure 4.1 Digital voice recorder. (Courtesy Olympus)

Another format for recording digital audio on a portable device is a mini-disc player-recorder. Sony makes the most popular recorders (see Figure 4.2), primarily designed as devices for downloading and playing music.

Figure 4.2 MiniDisc recorder/player. (Courtesy Sony Electronics)

These MiniDisc devices allow you to record audio files from a PC and transfer the files onto MiniDisk media that hold over five hours of music (when recording in LP4 mode). The mini-discs cost under $2 apiece and can be rerecorded. An advantage of this device over traditional MP3 players is that you can create quite a large library of mini-discs and carry many hours of audio around with the player. MP3 players do not have any removable device, so the only way to get new audio into them is to hook them back up to your computer, remove files, and download new ones. Although mini-disc recorders are primarily designed as music players, they do have a microphone jack that allows them to work like a voice recorder.

There are also devices for PDAs for recording audio (see Figure 4.3). Some handheld computers have built-in microphone in-jacks. For Handspring Visors, there are several devices that can slide into the expansion slot, like the Targus Total Recall Voice Recorder pictured here. This device records up to 90 minutes of audio with a built-in microphone; you can add an automatic date and time stamp. When you are finished, you can download the files to your PC, perform a sync operation, edit the files on your PC, and even e-mail the files as an attachment.

Figure 4.3 Audio recorder for a PDA. (Courtesy Handspring)

APPLICATIONS

How many times have you been met with a client or subject matter expert and wished you could have captured exactly what was said? With these small devices, you can easily record a conversation and then download it to your computer, file it, and even (with some units) convert the interview into a word processed document. This can be a very useful application for client meetings, for interviewing to collect materials for training or documentation, or for capturing user reactions to prototype materials. You can also use them to record noises that may be critical to include in training or documentation. Let's say that a motor makes a grinding sound when it is not properly lubricated or that a safety device emits a particular warning sound depending on what is detected. You can capture those sounds and include them in training courses or electronic documentation or even use them to play back during a classroom presentation by attaching them to a PowerPoint presentation.

To aid in troubleshooting and collaboration, you can deploy these devices within the organization, and employees or customers can simply talk out their thoughts (useful for those who do not or cannot type) or record unusual noises. These small files can then be e-mailed to a help line or to colleagues.

DIGITAL CAMERAS

Digital cameras are popular consumer devices and available at prices similar to those of traditional film cameras. The advantage of digital cameras is that you can immediately see what you have taken so it eliminates the unpleasant surprises of having film developed, only to find that the shot you needed was too dark or out of focus. You can also save a lot of money because you choose to print out only the pictures you want. In many cases, you may not need to print them at all; rather, you can share them electronically by sending them by e-mail or embedding them in Web sites or electronic documents.

Most people use stand-alone digital cameras, like the Sony Mavica pictured in Figure 4.4. However, there are other cameras that are designed to attach to PDAs, like the Eyemodule (see Figure 4.5). This tiny camera, about the size of a matchbox, slides into the expansion slot on a Handspring Visor and allows you to take color pictures and tiny movie files. Like the audio devices for a PDA, the photos taken with an Eyemodule are downloaded automatically to your PC whenever your perform a sync operation. From there, the graphics can be edited, e-mailed, or included in a Web page.

Figure 4.4 MVC-CD200 CD Mavica digital still camera. (Courtesy Sony Electronics, Inc.)

Figure 4.5 Eyemodule for Handspring Visor. (Courtesy www.eyemodule.com)

You can even get a camera to wear on your wrist. Casio makes a camera watch that takes pictures that get downloaded using a cable to your PC, or you can "beam" them to another Casio camera watch using its infrared port (see Figure 4.6). It can even store 100 black-and-white pictures.

Digital cameras range in price from about $60 to over $800, so it is important to understand some of the basic parameters. They use electronic chips that work as sensors to detect and process incoming light and convert it to a digital file. Camera sensors are rated in terms of megapixels—that is, millions of pixels (the little dots that make up the picture).

The more megapixels there are, the better the resolution of the picture and the larger the final printed picture will be.

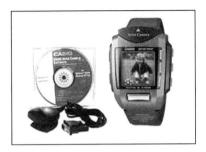

Figure 4.6 Wristwatch camera. (Courtesy Casio)

The cheapest cameras capture about 300,000 pixels— usually 640 rows and 480 columns, or 640 x 480. This will be adequate when reproduced on a computer but will not compare well to traditional film when printed out.

Most people are buying 2- and 3-megapixel cameras: 2-megapixel cameras have a resolution of 1600 x 1200 or higher, which is comparable to a film camera. For high-quality prints of 11 x 14 or larger, you'll need a 3-megapixel camera or even a professional digital camera that captures 6 million pixels (this kind costs about $10,000).

Resolution is probably the most important variable, but another factor to look at is focus and zoom options and lenses. Cheaper cameras have a fixed-focus lens; users cannot manually adjust the focus. This is fine for typical head-and-shoulders shots of people or landscapes, but not good for extreme close-ups or for choosing which of several objects in a scene should be in focus. An autofocus lens can adjust, but it does it manually with a little motor; the user has no control of it.

Digital cameras can have optical zoom or digital zoom. In optical zoom mode, the camera uses lenses that get longer or shorter to make the subject appear closer or farther away, just like on a traditional zoom lens camera. A digital zoom does a similar trick electronically: It takes the picture with a normal lens setting and then digitally enlarges it. The resulting zoomed-in picture is of lower quality because it enlarges just a portion of what the lens and sensor have captured. Pictures taken with a digital zoom are often not very presentable because of this.

Most cameras allow you to choose the resolution of pictures. Like audio files, you can choose high resolution but fewer pictures can be stored, or vice versa. You can choose the resolution of each picture as you take it, and they are normally stored in the JPEG format, a common file standard for editing and posting on Web pages. Almost all cameras have a built-in LCD screen that allows you to see what you are shooting and to display pictures so you can sort and edit them. Some very inexpensive cameras have no screen, so you've got to shoot and hope for the best until you can download them to a PC.

A final consideration when choosing digital cameras is memory. The cheaper cameras just have internal memory; when you fill it up, you must download to a computer or delete pictures to make room. The better cameras have removable media, so that you can just insert another memory card when you have filled one up. Because they are reusable, you will not need many of them unless you are traveling away from a computer for a very long time. Most cameras that use removable media come with an 8 megabyte (MB) or 16 MB memory card. A 16 MB card holds roughly 32 pictures at 1600 x 1200 resolution using normal JPEG compression. Most digital cameras either use SmartMedia or CompactFlash cards, which are about the size of a coin; the expensive ones can hold 250 MB. Other formats for storing picture files are the standard floppy disk that Sony uses on many of its cameras; the advantage here is that you can simply pop the floppy disk in your computer. However, floppy discs hold only 1.4 MB. Sony also has created the MemoryStick storage device, a solid-state device about the size of a stick of gum that holds up to 64 MB of data. However, it's a relatively expensive storage medium and works primarily with Sony devices; its Clié handheld computer and some of its laptops also accept MemorySticks.

To transfer files from the camera to a computer, most people connect up with a USB cable or a serial cable. There are adapters that let you plug a digital storage card right into your computer and use it like a tiny external floppy drive.

Up Close

Interview with
Donald R. Specker, Field Sales Agronomist,
Pioneer HiBred International, Ithaca, New York

Digital photos can be used for training and collaboration in the workplace. Donald Specker uses this technology with e-mail for fast and cost-effective instruction.

Briefly describe what device you are using and what the applications consist of. I work with a network of fifty or more sales representatives across seven northeastern states. Although it is preferable to communicate and educate in a one-on-one setting, it is not possible given the size of the area. I instituted a weekly electronic learning forum to get people in the habit of regular electronic communication and as a way to learn. Learning exercises consist of two multiple-choice questions per week, with the answers provided and explained the following week. I have also incorporated the use of digital images in the forum. Digital photographs of field crop challenges can be posed to the group as a learning tool [see Figure 4.7]. Some sales reps have secured digital cameras and have sent photographs to the group.

Figure 4.7 Using digital photos for crop analysis. (Courtesy Pioneer Hi-Bred International)

What got you started in using the mobile device or devices?
A desire to have regular contact and regular learning. The traditional method was to hold large, centralized meetings a few times a year and then go the route of "slug-feeding learning." A bite-size approach seemed like a better method. The habit of using electronic media also transfers to other business tasks the sales reps must complete, like invoicing and supply.

What have been the business or productivity results?
Although there have been no formal measurements of learning or productivity, there have been many instances where the sales reps have exhibited an increased level of knowledge.

Explain exactly how the application is created and then used by the end user. Explain what software or programming language is used, what team created this, and how the user gets it and manipulates it on his or her device.
Everything is prepared using standard Windows-based software. Communications are via Microsoft Outlook. Digital images are created as JPEG files and attached to the text document. Other attached documents are usually Microsoft Word files. Everyone

is on the company's internal e-mail system. A minimal amount of time is required, and standard software and digital cameras are used.

What were the biggest challenges or unexpected hurdles? As with any other adult education endeavor, there are challenges in participation and also addressing the diverse skill levels of the group. Our sales representatives are not employees, and it is not possible to mandate their involvement in the exercise. Despite these challenges, participation has been good, and the skill level of sales representatives is becoming higher and more uniform.

What are your future plans for mobile devices applications for training or business communications with your employees, students, and customers? I will continue using the weekly electronic forum. As a company, we have instituted a Web-based version of our popular *Walking Your Fields* newsletter, named *Scanning Your Fields*. It offers immediate communication of information to our customers. Sales representatives also have access to numerous intranet-based information sources.

What advice would you give to fellow training, business performance, and communications professionals with regard to getting into the use of mobile devices? Do not hesitate. The technology is simple and fits the way we all must communicate and practice business as we move ahead.

VIDEO CAMERAS

Although a still picture may well be worth a thousand words, video clips can be even more powerful media for capturing processes or unusual events. A large percentage of consumers own camcorders, so this section does not focus on general functions. Nevertheless, it is important to understand the difference between analog and digital video. Most camcorders, along with VCRs, produce and play back analog data. You can see the pictures on a TV set but cannot view them or manipulate them on a computer without digitizing the video and audio first. Video and audio capture cards that you can add on to a computer will allow you to do this. However, you can also start out by recording digital video.

Digital camcorders are a better choice than analog camcorders for professionals in training and performance improvement for several reasons (see Figure 4.8):

❐ You can directly upload the video to a computer using a FireWire port, a special high-speed connection. From your computer, you can edit the video and e-mail clips.

❐ The images do not degrade like analog tapes do when you make copies of them. With analog tapes, if you make a copy of a copy, every generation winds up with much poorer quality in terms of image stability and resolution (it's like making a copy of a copy on an office copier machine). With digital video, you can make endless copies, and they all look the same (like when you save or copy word processing files onto floppy disks; the copies are as good as the original).

❐ Digital video is easier to categorize, browse, search, and edit. Many camcorders automatically produce thumbnails, or small still pictures of the beginning and end frames of each scene shot. You can quickly index and mark segments, and with the DVD format, you never have to wait for tapes to fast-forward and rewind. With digital video editing, you can cut and paste scenes just as you cut and paste words and images in word processing.

Digital camcorders can be broken down into three categories based on the medium they use to store the data: mini-DV, Digital8, and DVD.

Mini-DV, the most common, uses tiny tapes (about one-twelfth the size of a standard VHS tape) so the camcorders

Figure 4.8 DCR-PC9 Handycam camcorder. (Courtesy Sony Electronics, Inc.)

themselves tend to be quite small. These tapes can hold up to two hours of information, with good resolution (about 500 lines). The Digital8 format is very similar to an 8 mm or Hi8 camcorder, and although it records digitally, it can play back analog 8 mm and Hi8 videos, which is a useful feature. It provides one hour of recording time at up to 500 lines of resolution.

The newest format for camcorders is DVD. A DVD is a digital videodisc, a CD-ROM–sized disc, used mostly for playing back movies. The CD-ROM player in your computer may be DVD compatible, and you have probably seen DVDs for rent in video rental stores. Like the other formats, it has 500 lines of resolution and can record up to two hours. One big advantage of DVD over tape is that the viewer can immediately jump to any scene without having to wait for fast-forwarding and rewinding. And since more computers are coming equipped with DVD players, it's a great distribution medium.

Camcorders range from under $1,000 to over $20,000, depending on features. The less expensive camcorders have one chip; the high-end professional ones use three chips and produce better color and resolution. There are several considerations when choosing a camcorder besides price:

Size. They can range from tiny devices that fit in a pocket to large cameras that look like broadcast news gear. The small ones are convenient, but sometimes they are so small that it's difficult to keep the camera steady. Slightly larger cameras that can rest on your shoulder may produce better images and be easier to hold.

Light sensitivity. Camcorders adjust automatically for light conditions, but some perform better under low light conditions or reproduce color more accurately under a wide range of lighting conditions, such as under the fluorescent lights common in offices and plants. Some have built-in lights.

Lens. Generally, the larger the lens is, the better the quality is. Look for cameras that have a good optical zoom range. Like digital still cameras, many camcorders offer digital zoom, but this actually just blows up all the pixels, making for very grainy-looking pictures when you zoom in.

Signal-to-noise ratio. The signal-to-noise (S/N) ratio refers to the amount of detail versus the amount of grain "noise" in a picture. The amount of noise can vary widely even within the same camera depending on how much "gain" or sensitivity it requires to try to make a picture in low lighting conditions. The lower the lighting, the higher the gain and the more noise. Consumer DVD cameras have S/N ratios in the low fifties; high-end professional cameras are in the sixties.

Digital stabilization. This feature automatically minimizes the jerkiness of any movement when you try to handhold a camera without a tripod.

Still picture capture. Many camcorders enable you to take stills, but you should check to see what the resolution is. Five hundred lines of resolution is fine for video but does not offer good resolution when you try to make an 8 x 10 still print. Some camcorders offer a memory card to save the still images, so that you can plug it directly into a computer peripheral to download them.

NONLINEAR EDITING

Although you may be able to use unedited video clips as short how-to's or as personal documentation, you will need to edit the video for any longer or more formal application. Digital video editing is called *nonlinear editing*, which means that you do not necessarily have to build the final edited piece from the beginning to the end, as you had to with traditional analog editing (think of writing an article on a typewriter, where it was impossible to insert text in the middle of something already written). Nonlinear editing allows you to create a video as you create a word processed document: You can start anywhere and add or subtract in the beginning, middle, or end until you're satisfied with the end result.

Editing software allows you to select just the parts of master or raw unedited video, assemble the cuts in any order, add special effects such as dissolves or fancy wipes, superimpose titles, and add various audio tracks. Although editing itself is quite an art, the software is relatively easy to manipulate.

Many organizations are using digital cameras and editing to capture motion clips for training and documentation, then distributing them via their intranets. For example, Intel uses the accelerated breakthrough system (ABS) to identify and videotape best practices of experts. This allows their training department to capture "tacit knowledge"—the skills and know-how that master performers have but often cannot articulate. By quickly videotaping their processes and posting them to the intranet, Intel can replicate master performance throughout its various manufacturing facilities.

•

Scanners

Another input device, perhaps less glamorous than wristwatch cameras and movie editing software, is the scanner. Scanners look like desktop copiers; you put a page or book in the top on a pane of glass, and a scanning element makes a digital image of it. This is useful for grabbing images, but scanning can do more. If you have a lot of printed material that you need to reuse (such as existing documentation or manuals) and you do not have the original word processing files, you can use optical character recognition (OCR) technology to avoid retyping.

To use OCR, you need special OCR software, but simple applications like this often come bundled with the scanner. When you begin the scan, you set up the parameters in the software to optimize the scan for recognizing text (this usually requires a very fine level of reproduction but no color). The scanner first makes a digital image, and then the OCR software tries to recognize the fonts and turns the graphic into a word processing document. Most software is about 98 percent accurate, which means that you will get a few mistakes in every page that you'll need to clean up by hand. OCR works best with very simple layouts. Many OCR packages cannot figure out what to do with text that wraps around pictures or is in columns or uses fancy fonts.

Handheld scanners are wonderful devices that fit in a pocket. They are about the size of a thick pen and allow you to scan in text line by line. Instead of an ink cartridge, they have a scanning head, and along the pen body is a small screen that can display a few lines of text. To use them, you scan over a document line by line and the software automatically does OCR. Then you save the document to the scanning pen's internal memory and upload it to a computer using a cable or infrared beam. Let's say that you are doing some observation of customer service representatives for a training needs analysis. You notice that one of them has developed a job aid that she has posted on her desk that would be a useful basis for a handout. Instead of copying it and then having to retype it, you can scan it in to the scanner pen and upload it to a computer later. Or if you're in a doctor's waiting room reading a magazine and come across a terrific quote for your next presentation, you can capture the text (and not have to steal the magazine!).

Most of these also come with built-in dictionary software, and you can also buy additional dictionaries, such as foreign language translators or medical terminology manuals that can be uploaded. As the users read, they can scan over words that they do not understand and get a definition on the screen. They can be used as a tiny pocket organizer by uploading names, addresses, and other small memos from a computer, and you can then display individual files on the scanner—just like a PDA but even smaller.

MULTIPURPOSE DEVICES

As mobile technology develops, we are starting to see a number of input devices that combine several functions. Instead of taking a digital audio recorder, scanner, PDA, and camera on the road, you may be able to take just one multi-function device. The models for these change as fast as the weather here in upstate New York, so I'll provide just a few descriptions of devices that are on the market now.

Ricoh has introduced a digital camera that wirelessly connects to the Web (see Figure 4.9). With it, you can take pictures, immediately upload them to the Web, and browse Web pages. Imagine, for example, an insurance agent being able to capture digital pictures of damage to a client's home, uploading that information immediately, and then browsing the Web for job aids or online forms to complete the transaction.

Figure 4.9 Ricoh camera and Web browser.

Another interesting combination device is the Kodak MC3 digital camera and MP3 player. It is aimed at a consumer market for people who want to take pictures and listen to music all in one device (the advertising pictures typically show teenagers taking pictures of parties and listening to their favorite tunes). But it would be a terrific device for sharing knowledge—for example, in a manufacturing facility where technicians could capture and share pictures of unusual situations or new devices and then listen to audio clips that explain the procedures.

UP CLOSE

Interview with
Keith Bohanan, Location Manager,
Paramount Television, Los Angeles

Imagine being able to instantly show your clients or trainees across the globe just what you are seeing now. Visual, mobile, wireless messaging is a powerful tool for productivity. Read how Hollywood is using it.

As a scout manager, you're in a position not unlike that of many training producers who need to find locations to shoot video or still pictures for training courses. Tell us a bit how your mobile media device helps you do your job. As a location scout and manager for a television series, I am as mobile as one can get. I drive around looking for filming locations. I am using one of the most exciting devices that I am aware of that exists today: the Ricoh 1-700 Digital Camera. This digital camera works with a Sprint Air Card. Together, the two devices work together as one. The digital camera allows me to be at a location and instantly e-mail a photograph to my home office, where a producer looks at the photograph and makes a decision at that moment about whether this is a location we would like to use for our show.

I started using mobile devices because I felt they would save an enormous amount of time. Time really is money, and for my business sometimes time is even more important than money.

In order to understand the benefit of the Ricoh 1-700 Digital Camera, you need an idea of how my job was performed before the I-700. I would get a script, read through it, and then head out in my car and start to photograph possible locations that I felt would make good candidates for that episode. I would then drive to each location, photograph it, and end my day at the film lab.

I would then wait the usual hour and a half at the 30-minute photo lab, get my photos, drive to my office, and start to tape together the photographs into separate folders for each location. The next morning, I would show these folders to the production designer, the producers, and the director. We would then narrow our choices to about three locations to drive out to and then choose which one, if any, would work for the show. As we would look at the locations, we would often get a call from the main office letting us know that a storyline had changed, requiring us to find another location. We then would end up driving back to the main office, and I would head back out and shoot new photos. I would then drive back to the 30-minute photo lab, wait my usual hour and a half, get my photos, drive back to the office, tape up my photos into folders, and the next morning we would have a meeting, look at the new choices, and then load up into the van, visit the new choices, and, yes, pick one.

That process has been turned into an amazing new way of doing things. I get my script, read through and break it down, get in my car, drive to choice A, shoot it with the Ricoh I-700, instantly e-mail it to the office, where the director and producer and production designer are working on other things but waiting for my call. They then check the photos of the location while I am on the cell phone with them. If they like it, then I shoot my film and hold onto it, then move on to the next location, and so on. By the end of the first day, we have a very good idea of what we will look at the next day, when we will lock in locations. This usually did not happen until the fourth day in the past.

The productivity results are enormous. We have cut our preparation time in half. This camera also has reinvented parts of film production for the show I work on. Time is usually a luxury we do not have. Some departments use the lack of time to their advantage. In the past, a set decorating department would dress a set, and the next day, when the director showed up, he or she would be more or less stuck with what was there. Now, with the Ricoh I-700, someone can shoot a photo of the set and e-mail it to the office, where it is printed for the director.

What were the biggest challenges you had in using the device? The biggest challenge was taking the time to learn and understand all the tools that this camera had to offer. I read all three manuals and have used most of the tools the I-700 has to offer. My future plans for mobile devices will include the Ricoh I-700 and any newer, faster data transfer devices that become available.

What advice do you have for others who might like to use new digital mobile devices? The best advice I would give to anybody using mobile devices is to be patient and learn what the device has to offer. This will take time and require reading the manual. The other part of being patient is that mobile devices are at the mercy of what path of data transfer you are using. Just like a cell phone that does not work in certain areas or drops your call, mobile devices have the same problems. As data transfer improves, so will the speed and performance.

DIGITAL OUTPUT DEVICES

I remember when it took a van load of equipment to conduct my workshops on interactive media: VCRs the size of small refrigerators, "portable" computers the size of a sewing machine, videodisc players, interface cards, separate monitors for video and computer playback, and hundreds of cables. Now I complain about having to lug a six-pound laptop and a portable projector about the same weight. Although laptops and modern LCD projectors are portable, they are not inexpensive. So if you are looking for devices that can display pictures, video, or sound to a group, you should explore some new alternatives. For example, you may support a sales team and want to enable sales reps to make electronic slide presentations for customers and for regional sales managers to show spreadsheets and Web pages at their weekly meetings with sales associates. Or you may want a mechanism to display a series of still pictures on a video screen and not have to use slides or computer projectors.

A number of options are emerging that allow you to use digital cameras and PDAs as media display devices. Perhaps the easiest is to use a digital camera instead of the old carousel slide tray. Most digital cameras allow you to edit a series of photos, even uploading images from a computer that may have been manipulated, with certain areas highlighted or titles superimposed. You then compose your slide show in the camera, and use the video-out jack that most of these have to connect directly to any TV set.

There are a few interesting software and hardware products that allow you to display PowerPoint or other documents on a PDA. Let's say that you want to deliver an electronic slide presentation but do not have a projector. With the powerViewer 2000 program, you can save the slide show on a PDA and beam it to other PDA users, either to look at on their own screens as you deliver your presentation or as a leave-behind. To use a conventional computer projector to display slides, Web pages, Word documents, or anything else from the screen of a Handspring Visor, you can use Presenter-to-Go (see Figure 4.10). This device fits in

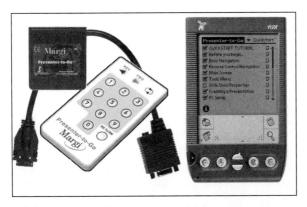

Figure 4.10 Presenter-to-Go allows you to show PowerPoint presentations from your Visor. (Courtesy MARGI Systems)

the Springboard expansion slot on a Visor and allows you to download PowerPoint presentations or documents into its own memory and then attach the Visor directly to a computer projector to display and control your show from your PDA. The laptop is not needed. The display is impressively sharp (1024 x 768); the only caveat here is that the memory is limited (about 2 MB), so huge PowerPoint shows do not fit. And because a considerable current is required to drive the VGA output to a computer projector, the device needs to be powered by an AC adapter.

CHECKLIST FOR EVALUATION AND LAUNCH OF DIGITAL INPUT AND OUTPUT DEVICES

❏ Develop a compelling case for capturing, indexing, and sharing audiovisual material. Here are some important uses:

❏ Capturing best practices or "how-to's" for training needs analysis, instructional design, knowledge management systems, or documentation

❏ Putting cheap audiovisual capture devices in the hands of performers themselves so that they can do ongoing documentation of work processes

❏ Being able to support on-the-job training with small handheld devices like showing visuals using a digital camera or PDA

❏ Creating fast transcriptions of interviews done during needs analysis, interviewing of subject matter experts, or posttraining assessment

❏ Look into what file standards are used within your company already for digital audio, still picture, and video files. Select a device and software that are compatible.

❏ Consult online shopping guides for the latest specs and comparisons among competing products. Do not necessarily buy the most feature-rich product; it may be harder to use than simpler ones.

❏ Make sure you buy a device that uses standard file formats and storage media so that you do not wind up with an "orphaned" system; also check into the pricing of storage media because that will become an important item in the overall budget.

❏ Think about creating easily accessible databases for your audio and video files; if they are Web-enabled applications, then other users can quickly reuse your materials for other purposes or check out files for quick reference.

RESOURCES

www.cnet.com, an excellent source for comparison shopping for digital media devices and software

www.znet.com, a great central source for comparison shopping as well as quick tutorials on how to create various digital media

www.margi.com, manufacturers of Presenter-to-Go hardware for the Handspring Visor to display presentations directly from a PDA to a computer projector

www.ibrite.com, vendor for powerViewer to show and distribute PowerPoint on a PDA

Your Pad
or Mine?

Tablets,

Webpads, and

Ruggedized

Notebooks

BACK **IN** 1996, I saw an ad for a Compaq Concerto computer and knew that I had seen the future of computing. The Concerto was a small, elegant laptop computer with a detachable keyboard. The screen was touch sensitive and could run any Windows-compatible software—and it could be run entirely by touching the screen with a finger or the stylus. It included a form of handwriting recognition and some simple calendar and note-taking applications. I ran out and bought one and loved it, although soon the product was an orphan. The handwriting recognition was a bit too clumsy and inaccurate, and the idea of keyboardless computing was before its time.

The Concerto was not the first pen-based computer. In the early 1990s, Go Corporation developed a pen-based operating system called PenPoint. When that failed to reach any market penetration, Windows 95 came out with an add-on called Pen Services and a version called Windows for Pen Computing. A number of manufacturers came up with innovative pen-based computers, including the pioneering Grid computer, but basically the idea of handwriting recognition and pen-based applications really never caught on until the Palm Pilot was introduced. Both the size of the Palm Pilot and the stability of the Graffiti alphabet for writing with a stylus finally enabled this technology to find its own niche.

DESCRIPTION OF DEVICES

Although the Palm Pilot and its counterpart PDAs have made a major impact on business computing, the screens are too small and the processors too weak for many applications. That's where tablet and pen-based computers, Webpads, and rugged notebook computers come in. Here's a brief description of these devices:

	Form Factor	Operating System, Applications
Ruggedized laptops	These are basically conventional laptops in terms of size and function, but they are built for harsh environments so that they have shock-resistant components and may be waterproof with heavy-duty screens. Many have rugged and brightly painted integral cases so that they are easy to spot and not as susceptible to theft.	Versions of Microsoft Windows.
Tablet and pen-based computers	These look like laptop computers with the keyboard section removed. Designed for input by touch screen or stylus, they have a sensitive screen and may have several physical buttons around the device to access features instantly.	Most of these run conventional Windows or Windows CE operating systems, although some Linux products are emerging.
Webpads	An emerging category of devices that are designed around wireless "always-on" capability and stylus input. Many have handwriting recognition built in and can range in size from a traditional laptop (minus the keyboard) down to something the size of a thick business card. Some are basically laptops without a keyboard, and some, like the POGO, are cell phones with an enhanced display and small tablet design rather than a handset design.	They may use conventional operating systems or be built around proprietary standards.

Bill Gates's keynote address at the fall 2000 COMDEX conference featured Microsoft's Tablet PC initiative, and he followed that up with a presentation at the WinHEC conference for software developers in 2001 where he called the Tablet PC "one of the coolest Microsoft innovations" (see

Figure 5.1). The prototype he displayed was thin and light, like a pad of paper; it booted up almost instantly with Windows XP Professional and had a high-resolution screen. Using an application called MS Notebook, you can write on the screen, which immediately displays a smooth flow of "ink," sampling the location of the pen over 130 times a second. You can make sketches, or the application can recognize your handwriting and turn it into word processing. You can cut and paste, undo, search, and highlight your handwritten notes using easy commands, just as with conventional word processing.

Figure 5.1 Tablet PC for the Road Warrior. (Courtesy Panasonic)

A number of manufacturers are developing tablet PCs and Webpads. In addition to the use of a pen or stylus on the screen, almost all of them feature wireless connectivity built in. For example, the POGO device uses the GSM (global systems for mobiles) cell network to transmit and display compressed high-quality graphics. Squeezed into the tiny device are a mobile phone, MP3 player, Web Browser, and Text Messenger, along with the basic suite of personal information management software (see Figure 5.2).

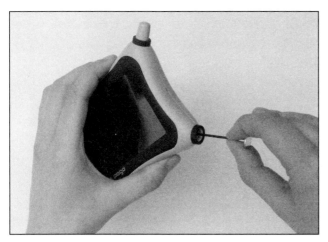

Figure 5.2 Webpad. (Courtesy Pogo Technology Ltd., www.pogo-tech.com)

Although the technology is changing quickly, there are already some significant applications for tablet computers, specifically for users who do not work at a desk but need a more feature-rich device than a small PDA.

APPLICATION FOR INTEGRATED DATA GATHERING

One of the most competitive and rapidly changing industries in the United States is the energy utility market, and one of the companies leading the transformation is Florida Power and Light (FPL), the utility that supplies power to more than 7 million customers in eastern and southern

Florida. It initiated Technology 21, a large project to revamp its information infrastructure completely, and a key part of this was extending mobile computing to its field repair force.

In November 2000, about 400 of FPL's repair trucks were outfitted with Fujitsu PenCentra tablet computers and wireless connections. These devices are about the size of a small clipboard and have 8-inch screens; they run an application called Advantex that schedules and routes the crews to their locations. This application is coupled with new wireless utility meters that are being installed at customers' buildings and homes. The system greatly streamlines the repair and connection processes, eliminating paperwork and lots of middlemen between the customer and repair technician.

Similar applications are being used by SBC Communications (formerly known as Southwestern Bell) for its service technicians. It initiated a project called Technicians of the Future, centering on developing a sophisticated and integrated mobile device that incorporates work flow management, testing equipment, job aids, and mapping software. Today, SBC technicians carry intelligent field devices: specially equipped, ruggedized computers (see Figure 5.3). They no longer have to carry a line tester; the VIP Sidekick application displays the condition of the telephone line via a series of on-screen gauges with data captured from a line tester that plugs into the computer's device bay. The computer is also used for scheduling and documenting work on jobs, and a mapping program shows the location of all of the organization's assets in the field. Most interesting from a performance standpoint, the Trouble Pro application captures and disseminates the knowledge of an experienced lineman. This expert system–job aid walks a technician through the troubleshooting process, recommending solutions to the most common repair problems.

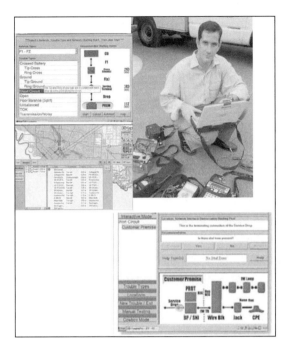

Figure 5.3 SBC technicians use ruggedized laptops for troubleshooting, testing, and scheduling and finding repair locations. (Courtesy Panasonic)

TABLET COMPUTERS AND JOB AIDS

Back in the mid-1990s, hospital administrators were striving for solutions to maximize physicians' and nurses' productivity while minimizing costs. These professionals are very mobile within their work environment and constantly record and retrieve vital patient information to and from a myriad of sources. The time required for all this limits the physician's ability to focus attention on the patient. Some hospitals began using tablet computers to access network servers remotely to document and retrieve patient data. Using a wireless connection, they could instantly update information while having the freedom to roam about the hospital. Emergency room physicians could use a patient management system to interview and examine patients and simultaneously enter data into their desktop computers using the CruisePad. They could also retrieve patient vital signs and laboratory and X-ray results, as well as view real-time electrocardiogram monitoring from patients elsewhere within the hospital. For complex patient diagnoses, they could use the CruisePad to dial up an online medical library or access a medical CD-ROM library while visiting with a patient. Prior to admitting or discharging a patient, physicians could review drug interactions, create instructions, update anatomical illustrations, and write and print prescriptions. If necessary, they could even print charts for later pickup or even send faxes.

There were some limitations: These early tablet computers had a relatively small transmission radius (about 500 feet), and occasionally the connection between host and mobile computer would be severed—for example, when going through a lead-cased radiology department. They also had limited battery life and unreliable handwriting recognition.

The use of tablet computers dropped in the late 1990s because of limitations like these, but interest is escalating. One of the big drivers is actually an outgrowth of the PDA market. Many organizations that saw the benefits of mobile computing with PDAs ran into limitations of power and screen size with some of their intended applications. While maintaining the mobility and input ease of a PDA, tablet computers provide bigger screens, better resolution, and more computing power and storage. One of those PDA-to-tablet migration stories is the TKM (Total Knowledge Management) System developed by Generation21 Learning Systems.

Up Close

Interview with
Dale Zwart, CTO and Founder,
Generation21 Learning Systems, Golden, Colorado

Knowledge management initiatives exist in most large corporations, but many of them have been stymied by high costs and reluctant users. Generation21 has found a way to deliver vital information using tablet PCs.

Briefly describe what device you are using and what the applications consist of. The TKM system can deliver chunks of information that support employees on the job via handheld devices and tablet computers. TKM's ability to deliver just-in-time information, in addition to instructional graphics and links to text-based learning objects, sets it apart from other e-learning products that integrate wireless functionality. Now, off-site employees can access their organization's entire database of knowledge, search out specific learning objects, and get the instructional graphics or data they need to complete tasks, answer customer questions, and locate procedures. We call it Instant Knowledge.

What got you started in using the mobile device or devices? Generation21 customers understand that their field service team members are their primary connections to customers. We created TKM's Instant Knowledge capabilities to ensure that remote workers could respond quickly to customers' demands. That translates into consistent revenue growth, enhanced customer loyalty, and high-quality referrals.

In addition, Instant Knowledge quickly proved itself as a way for organizations to reconnect with their field service team members. And when remote workers have the same access to knowledge that the rest of the organization does, morale increases, employee-management relations improve, and, consequently, the organization's productivity is enhanced.

Explain how the application is used. Who are the users, and what is the setting? In July 2000, PRI Automation became the first Generation21 client to adopt the wireless TKM Instant Knowledge functionality. PRI, a leader in advanced automation systems and software for the semiconductor industry, uses TKM to help employees maximize their full potential by harnessing knowledge for use in formal browser-based training events, as well as for on-demand, on-the-job performance support.

With TKM, PRI breaks its collective institutional knowledge and training materials down into right-sized "chunks" of information. Those chunks are then stored on a relational database, and employees can search for information at the very moment when they need it to answer a question or complete a task. Earlier versions of TKM provided this Instant Knowledge functionality via a desktop or laptop, but the wireless innovation introduced in recent versions of TKM is of particular benefit to PRI, as the organization wanted to support off-site technicians with knowledge in the same manner it does other employees.

While the majority of PRI's employees remain in-house to perform their jobs, they too benefit from the use of TKM's Instant Knowledge. A survey of some PRI employees indicated that many spend valuable time away from the job trying to find answers via phone, e-mail, face-to-face contact with colleagues, or in written documents. The value of having on-demand performance support capabilities at PRI became very clear: 90 percent of the survey participants said that they would use a hand-held computer to find their answers.

What have been the business or productivity results? PRI estimated that the malfunction of a product could cost customers almost $1,000 of lost profit per minute. Per incident, malfunctioning equipment and human error can cost in excess of $100,000. This is one of the main reasons that PRI uses Instant Knowledge to deliver the most current information on demand to field service engineers.

Using TKM, the organization shifted from the process of providing manuals, which were out of date the minute they were printed, to empowering technicians to access knowledge using wireless devices. By delivering information at the very moment when technicians need it and without forcing them to locate a manual, sift through the entire thing, and return to the job, PRI reduces the time it takes to make repairs and consequently saves its customers money.

PRI leverages knowledge to the greatest extent possible by delivering it right to learners at the point when they are most prepared to receive it. Whereas many companies focus on developing content solely for the purpose of formal training events, PRI continues to experience more significant gains in productivity through the blending of traditional training and Instant Knowledge that TKM provides [see Figure 5.4].

Figure 5.4 Example of the TKM system job aid screens.

Explain exactly how the application is created and then used by the end user. Explain what software or programming language is used, what team created this, and how the user gets it and manipulates it on his or her device. The Instant Knowledge system is a server-based wireless extension of TKM. It allows users to connect to a TKM server using wireless devices. Users can search indexes and use keyword searches to retrieve performance support documents from the TKM databases. The performance support documents are created dynamically; the system assembles the appropriate "chunks" of knowledge, called Universal Knowledge Objects (UKOs). The UKOs are always aware of their relationship to other objects in the database and when delivered to a user, can guide the user to the next step in a process, or advise the learner of any previous steps that he or she must understand before performing a task.

The server side system uses a number of technologies, including Web and application servers running on Windows and Unix platforms. On the handheld devices, standard browser and Web-clipping applications are used to support Instant Knowledge.

How long does it typically take to design and deploy such an application? Once an organization has content developed and published in the TKM system, it can be made available to employees immediately via wireless Instant Knowledge. Organizations can typically begin creating course work and delivering Instant Knowledge within days of implementing TKM.

What were the biggest challenges or unexpected hurdles? The objective of the wireless Instant Knowledge trials was to validate both the premise of our performance support model and the use of PDAs as a platform to deliver the content. We were successful in both respects. The search engine identified relevant content that met the needs of workers, and the PDA proved capable of handling the information streams.

The value of the wireless Instant Knowledge discovered during these trials exceeded our expectations. Users quickly embraced the concept of performance support and requested that the amount of content available be increased. During these initial trials, users also provided valuable recommendations for improvements and enhancements, including adding advanced media such as movie clips and animation (this enhancement has already been made), using the PocketPC platform (this enhancement has already been made), allowing users to save a document on the device, and adding synchronization support for frequently used reference documents.

What are your future plans for mobile devices applications for training or business communications with your employees and customers? Generation21 is working with PRI to move toward a media-rich version of its Instant Knowledge system. The next device that Generation21 will work with developing an Instant Knowledge performance support system is the Qbe, a tablet-like computer with a wireless card. We will continue to work on media-rich content that can be delivered without a lot of bandwidth.

What advice would you give to fellow training, business performance, and communications professionals with regard to getting into the use of mobile devices? Ensure that the technology you choose:

❏ Can deliver instructional graphics and links to text-based learning objects. Some systems do not support media.

❏ Is already in use within client organizations and is not merely in the testing or creation phases.

❏ Delivers the same information by wireless devices that it does by desktop or laptop computers. Information for both delivery methods should come from one development effort, so that information is consistent regardless of how it is accessed.

❏ Is provided by a vendor that is a long-term player in the market. Many new entrants were introduced into the wireless e-learning software market. Unfavorable equity and venture capital markets will decimate many of them, particularly the larger players that will require a secondary offering to remain viable.

How to Create Applications for Tablet Computers

The great thing about tablet PCs, ruggedized laptops, and most Webpads is that under their sleek faces, they are traditional PCs running conventional Windows-based software. This means that any program that can run on a regular desktop or laptop PC can run on a Webpad. There are a few caveats, of course. First, some tablet PCs do not have disk drives or CD-ROMs built in, so do not depend on those media for field use (some have external drives for installing programs but their use destroys the whole point of a single tablet device for handheld use). Second, not all tablet PCs have audio, so check before creating programs with sound or narration.

The form factor of tablet computers means that they are designed for stylus or touch-screen input. Although handwriting recognition is built in, it may not work well, so you need to design applications that use primarily buttons or "hot" areas. Many authoring programs can do this, but watch out for requirements for users to employ keyboard input, like Control or Function keys, or, for lots of accurate typing, the use of long user IDs and passwords.

Although Webpads are obviously designed for wireless Web access, the cellular infrastructure in North America is still far from flawless, so do not count on users being able to access online applications seamlessly, especially in rural areas or inside buildings.

CHECKLIST FOR EVALUATING AND LAUNCHING TABLET COMPUTING

Tablet PCs and Webpads are still mostly in prototype form. Although there are units available, new standards have just been set by Microsoft, and this fact will undoubtedly have a large impact on the next generation of tablets. Microsoft has indicated that the Tablet PC hardware platform specification will generally be pretty loose, meaning that the original equipment manufacturers will have a significant amount of leeway in determining exactly how they design their products. All that is known today about the Tablet PC hardware platform specification is that they must be thin and light and have a minimum processor speed of 400 MHz and at least 128 MB of memory in order to run Windows XP.

The screen digitizer that recognizes input must have a sampling rate of greater than 100 times per second, a battery life greater than 4 hours and no fan, and be able to resume from the suspend state almost instantly.

When thinking about or choosing a tablet PC, consider the following:

- ❏ Is there a need for a handheld keyboardless application?
- ❏ Can I create applications that rely mostly on "hot" buttons and areas on the screen?
- ❏ How will batteries be recharged in the field?
- ❏ Is wireless access required? If so, what is the standard used by the hardware, and is the connectivity (cellular) infrastructure available and reliable in the areas needed?
- ❏ Is the tablet rugged enough for the intended use (e.g., shockproof, waterproof, relatively scratchproof screen?)

RESOURCES

www.mobilemania.com, a source for tablet PCs and related support and software

www.pencomputing.com, for PenComputing Magazine; a great source for articles on this technology

www.pogo-tech.com, for POGO Webpad

www.frontpath.com, ProGear Internet appliance

www.transmetazone.com, for the company that manufactures components for tablet PCs and Webpads and has links to vendors and opinion and technical articles

6

No Strings Attached

Smart Cell Phones

and Other

Wireless

Connectivity

Teenagers **in** Japan flirt via mobile phone instant messaging; you can now buy a car that will let you speak into a wireless device to trade stocks while driving; and in May 2001, a minister in Berlin conducted a sermon via mobile phone for which 1,300 young people had signed up beforehand. Wireless connectivity, also called "pervasive" computing, will be a significant force in business and learning in the very near future. There are already about 50 million mobile workers in the United States alone, so the market for communications that does not require being tethered to a phone or network line is very attractive.

Over 400 million cell phones were sold worldwide in 2000, and many industry researchers predict that PDAs will be eclipsed by smart phones that combine the functions of a computer with traditional voice calls and an "always-on" connection to the Internet. Some high-tech market research firms expect that over the next several years, wireless devices will replace the PC as the preferred vehicle for accessing the Internet, with over 1.3 billion users worldwide.

Wireless is an important component of mobile learning and performance improvement, especially now that people have become accustomed to accessing large amounts of data that are centrally updated and stored and updated on Internet servers. There are two categories of wireless applications that are important to understand:

1. Wireless networks that use radio or infrared signals to allow computers and PDAs to connect to a local area network and Internet access

2. Telephony technologies that build on cellular phone and pager systems and add the ability to receive and send text (and sometimes graphical) information

WIRELESS NETWORKS

Both categories of wireless applications are important for training and performance improvement applications, but in different ways. Today, many offices, schools, and conference facilities are installing wireless networks. These allow users to carry around their laptops and PDAs and always be connected to the network without any physical connection to it. The computing devices generally use an add-on card inserted into either the PC card slot or an expansion slot on the PDA that receives the data; the network data are beamed out by transmitters, called *access points,* placed around the facility. An office worker can take her laptop from her office to a conference room, out to the cafeteria, and over to a coworker's desk without losing connection to the company network or the Internet. Or students can bring laptops into a school or training facility without needing to find a physical connection or stringing wires around. Apple, Dell, and some other computer manufacturers are now offering laptops with built-in antennas, so no added card is necessary.

There are several standards for wireless networking:

Standard	Maximum Range from Computer to Base Station	Speed of Transfer in Megabytes per Second (Mbps)
IEEE 802.11, the first popular wireless networking standard	1,200 feet	3 Mbps
IEEE 802.11b wireless (also called Wi-Fi for Wireless Fidelity), a new version, popular in corporate locations and public Internet access sites, that offers faster data speeds	150 feet	About 11 Mbps
Home RF, a cheaper wireless connection technology mostly aimed at home usage because it is easier to set up than the 802.11b standard; supports data transfer on one channel while another channel handles voice calls over cellular networks	100 feet	1.6 Mbps

Standard	Maximum Range from Computer to Base Station	Speed of Transfer in Megabytes per Second (Mbps)
HomeRF Shared Wireless Access Protocol (SWAP), a new standard that adds support for streaming audio and MPEG-1 video, as well as up to eight wireless phones	100 feet	4 Mbps
IEEE 802.15, also known as Bluetooth, is a wireless technology specification designed to enable wireless communication between small, mobile devices like laptops, PDAs, cell phones, printers, and digital cameras	Designed for short-range transmission (under 30 feet)	720 Kps

Most wireless LANs (local area networks) are designed to connect laptops, and there is a wide range of cards and built-in devices to support this. Now there are solutions that will allow PDAs to connect to wireless networks also. For example, Xircom has created a SpringPort Wireless Ethernet module that connects Handspring Visor PDAs to any 802.11b network (see Figure 6.1).

New wireless networking technologies will certainly emerge. One possibility is even the use of fluorescent lights to create an optical network. MIT professor Steven Leeb has developed a retrofit for ordinary office light fixtures that modulates light intensities that are not discernable to humans yet can transmit data through very rapid flickering.

Closer to our horizon—actually right on our horizon—is the Bluetooth standard, begun in 1994 by Ericsson and supported by more than 2,000 hardware manufacturers. Rather than being primarily a link between computers and a main server, it is a wireless standard for small portable devices so that they can connect with each other within about a 30-foot radius. It is designed primarily to avoid having to wire devices that need to "talk" to each other, like PDAs, printers, wireless keyboards, and cell phones. Any active Bluetooth device will automatically search for other Bluetooth devices in its immediate radius and can exchange appropriate files. For example, if you were giving a presentation on your Bluetooth-enabled laptop in a meeting, you could wirelessly send copies of it to others in the room with laptops or PDAs.

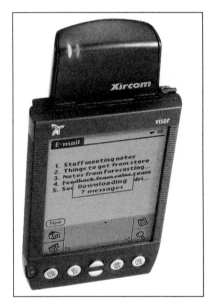

Figure 6.1 Wireless Ethernet module in PDA. (Courtesy Xircom)

But wireless networks are designed, at best, only for use within a building and its immediate surroundings. To get no-strings-attached connectivity beyond that, you need to look at smart cell phones.

CELLULAR PHONE STANDARDS

Almost every home has at least one cell phone user, if not more. With very attractive long-distance rate plans, many people are even opting to use their cell phones in lieu of traditional phone service, and many people in the workplace use their cell phones more frequently than their office phones.

It has become so easy to buy a cell phone and a service plan that most of us are unaware of the technology (actually, multiple technologies) behind the cell phones. When cell phones were introduced into North America, the vast majority of them used an analog system. After 1998, most of the cellular service providers began to switch over their services to digital cellular, which offers a clearer signal plus the ability to add features such as text messaging and even browsing the Web. The catch is that not all the digital systems are compatible, and most of them are not up to the task of delivering large amounts of graphical or even text information at an acceptable speed. There are several major cellular standards in the world today:

Standard	Application Information	Major Providers
CDMA (code division multiple access)	Cell phone standard predominantly used in the United States; supports voice and data, and users are generally charged by the minute	Sprint PCS, Verizon
CDPD (cellular digital packet data)	Wireless standard used for PDAs and text-based pagers with large coverage across the United States; generally provides service for flat fees	OmniSky, GoAmerica

Standard	Application Information	Major Providers
GSM (global standard for mobile communication)	Cellular technology used by most of Europe; not widely used in the United States	AT&T Wireless
TDMA (time division multiple access)	Cellular standard popular in the United States; supports voice but not data	Cingular
GPRS (general packet radio services)	A so-called 2.5-generation system that offers data rates of up to 115 Kbps	Likely to be used as an upgrade for GSM and TDMA operators
DoCoMo i-mode	An extremely popular cell phone standard used in Japan that allows for continuous connection to the Internet; it has over 25,00 content sites	

The problem with using any of the existing standards (called second generation, or 2G) is that the data rates are too slow for accessing even tiny Web-based applications or e-mail. Currently, providers like Sprint PCS provide data throughput of about 14.4 Kbps; 3G systems will provide about ten times that speed. The most successful advanced cell phone service in the world is DoCoMo in Japan, whose always-on system allows people to continuously chat online; it has more than 20 million users. The promise of m-commerce and other smart cellular applications is in the upcoming 3G systems that will require the installation of over $1 billion worth of infrastructure equipment by prospective service providers.

Cell phones that can display Web content are called Webphones or sometimes WAP phones (for wireless application protocol). Although the sites they display look just like Web sites, it is necessary to adapt Web content specifically for them because they have much smaller displays and very limited memory.

Form Factors for Smart Cell Phones

Delivering text messages is a challenge with conventional cell phone designs. Many current phones that have messaging services require using a very cumbersome method of typing letters—basically pressing the numerical keys several times to tap out the letters of the alphabet. Clearly, this cannot work for training and performance support applications.

New lines of smart phones, being introduced by most manufacturers, typically have larger displays than standard cell phones, and they have either keyboards or an area that uses some sort of handwriting recognition with a sensitive screen and a stylus (see Figures 6.2 and 6.3). Several phones are incorporating a Palm-compatible PDA into them, so that all the functions of an organizer and Graffiti handwriting recognition plus a cell phone are rolled into one unit.

Figure 6.2 Kyocera cell phone with a built-in Palm PDA. (Courtesy Kyocera Wireless)

Figure 6.3 Nokia cell phones with built-in keyboards. (Courtesy Nokia)

Yet another approach is to start with a PDA and add a cell phone. For example, you can get a tiny cell phone module that fits into the expansion slot of a Handspring Visor (see Figure 6.4). Several cell phone service plans are available for it, but they do not yet cover the entire United States.

Prototype cell phones are showing the innovative and tiny form factors that we may well see in the future. Figures 6.5 through 6.7 represent some designs that are being considered.

Figure 6.4 Handspring Visorphone.(Courtesy Handspring)

Figure 6.5 Prototype cell phone. (Courtesy Nokia)

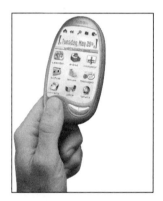

Figure 6.6 Another prototype. (Courtesy Nokia)

Figure 6.7 Cell phone prototype showing video transmission. (Courtesy Nokia)

CELL PHONES FOR TECHNICAL SUPPORT

It is easy to see how these innovative cell phones can be used to provide support to technical and sales people in the field. Even without considering futuristic designs and expensive plans, conventional cell phones with messaging services can make service calls much more efficient. For example, Ithaca College in upstate New York gives cell phones with Web browsing and e-mail capabilities to its computer technicians who are responsible for installation and repair throughout the campus. They can be immediately sent instructions telling them which job to go to next, and they can also send instant e-mail messages back to their main office. In the future, these Web-enabled phones will allow the technicians to call up information on the college's own computer support intranet pages and to access the Web pages of computer hardware and software vendors for up-to-date help.

CELL PHONES AND TRAINING

Can you imagine training via cell phone? It's being done today, and without exorbitant costs or technical miracles. In the following interview you'll see a great example of "blended learning": the use of multiple modalities for instruction. Course content was provided on Web and WAP-based cell phone platforms, allowing the course designers to incorporate text, coaching messages from instructors, questions and tutorials, and even video clips.

Up Close

Interview with
Geoff Ring, Academic Director,
ICUS PTE LTD, Singapore

INSEAD is widely recognized as one of the world's largest and most influential graduate business schools, with a tradition of innovation from its creation in 1957. It has twin campuses in Fontainebleau, France, and Singapore. It partnered with ICUS, a Singapore-based company specializing in creating e-learning, to create courses that use Web-enabled cell phones.

Briefly describe what device you are using and what the applications consist of. INSEAD, Nokia, and ICUS formed an Asia-Pacific consortium aimed at trialing mobile e-learning (m-learning). The initial result of their endeavors was the development and deployment of an e-learning course called "eBusiness on the Move" via the WAP-enabled 6210 Nokia phone. The course was developed to make use of both WAP (wireless) and Web (wired) technologies, allowing participants to access it through both phone and computer.

A tight integration of the course content and dual access for 70 percent of the course enabled participants to experience the same course by whatever combination of access means they chose. The progress of the students was tracked, and they received the normal level of ICUS coaching support and more than normal technical support because of the additional use of WAP technology.

INSEAD provided the course content, and ICUS applied proven online instructional design principles and a sound pedagogical approach to design an e-learning course [see

Figure 6.8]. Optimal use was made of the strengths of the WAP and Web technologies. Nokia provided technical WAP expertise and played an important role in marketing and mobile-related activities.

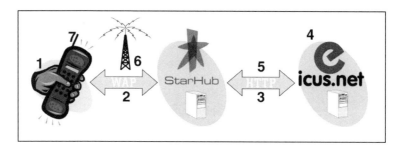

Figure 6.8 INSEAD technical infrastructure.

The course successfully introduced mobile Internet as a means of delivery for e-learning and provided participants with the opportunity to familiarize themselves with the mobile Internet environment. It also provided participants with an avenue to exchange ideas and experiences as well as an INSEAD certificate on successful completion of the course.

About 10 percent of the course was accessible via the WAP phone only, 20 percent via the Web only, and 70 percent via both delivery modes. The WAP 10 percent mainly included visits to WAP sites and quick reminders and alerts from the coach; the Web 20 percent mainly included digital video clips (one hour total), bulletin board activities, e-mail activities, and visits to Web sites.

What got you started in using the mobile device or devices? The course enabled the INSEAD executive education participants to take part in an e-learning course to communicate and exchange information using Internet and WAP technology, thus facilitating learning beyond the traditional boundaries of a fixed place and time. The course fee includes the materials, coaching, a Nokia WAP phone for the duration of the course, and the StarHub mobile plan with free local and data calls.

Explain how the application is used. Who are the users, and what is the setting? Participants were mainly senior executives or young successful businesspeople, typical of INSEAD's target population for its executive education courses. They typically had at least three years of work experience and were in an established position in senior management in a large corporation. In terms of technical skills, participants were expected to be competent users of the Internet for information gathering and for conducting online retail purchases.

The setting was a virtual one. In practice, the setting was anywhere in Singapore (for example, home, office, train, taxi). It was also available at the cost of a local call in Hong Kong and Malaysia via the telco's roaming facility.

What have been the business or productivity results? Further trials are needed to prove economic viability, although it is apparent that this will require a larger geographical market reach.

For ICUS and INSEAD, high-quality management training was available for businessmen and -women who could not take the time to participate in an INSEAD course in Singapore or France. The course delivery model was tailor-made to suit busy executives, enabling them to participate regardless of their location (within Singapore for Phase 1). It appealed to participants who otherwise could not participate in courses due to ever-changing schedule and extensive traveling. It also served as a high-technology showcase for familiarizing users with new WAP technology provided by Nokia.

For Nokia and its telecommunications partner (StarHub in Singapore), it provided extended WAP/VAS offerings for the corporate segment and new users and usage for current infrastructure. It also differentiated competitors in the valuable corporate customer segment and supported other VAS offerings and their usage (airtime, revenue).

Because the project was experimental, the results of Phase 1 were quantified only in terms of the research results obtained from a combination of survey and phone interviews with the business executive participants.

Prior to taking this course, only five of the fourteen participants expected to enjoy the experience of using the WAP
mobile phone for learning. This view was mainly based on
the belief that the screen was too small to be useful. Most
learners believed that they would make little use of the
phone. A typical view was, "Because of the phone's small
screen size, I expected to use the computer for almost
everything."

After the course, all participants were of the opinion that
the WAP-delivered content had added value to the learning
experience and that the "anywhere" access provided an
additional level of convenience.

Most students found it easy to read the material on the
phone screen, a fact that surprised them because they had
expected it to be more difficult. The most common uses
were for multiple-choice questions, coach reminders,
browsing content, and voice communications. Here are
some typical views:

> "The SMS [short messaging service] reminders from the
> coach were useful, especially for overdue assignments!"

> "The multiple choice quizzes with immediate feedback
> were excellent."

> "Browsing course material before doing computer activi-
> ties was helpful."

Nearly all participants were pleased with the overall quality of the course and also the content and technical expertise provided by their two coaches and the technical help
desk. Typical comments were:

> "Liked the fact that I could access material from home."

> "I would recommend the course to others. Apart from the
> time constraints, because of the bulletin board discus-
> sions, the course offered maximum flexibility."

> "I liked the activities and discussions."

"It was reassuring to have direct access to the coach for content issues and the help desk for technical issues."

"Excellent. Meant I could work from anywhere."

All students reported that they were able to navigate through the course easily using either the phone or the computer. Most students found it easy to determine where to begin again when they changed from the computer to the phone and vice versa. The hard copy comparison chart that linked the numerous phone "chunks" with the larger computer "topics" was found to be useful in this regard. Most learners reported that their opinion about the usefulness of the WAP/phone technology for learning was much more positive as a result of having experienced the course. Common comments about navigating through the WAP phone content were:

"The multilevel menu system was easy to follow."

"I could move around the content quicker on the phone."

Nevertheless, only about half the learners would have deemed the 80 percent of the course available via the WAP phone to be satisfactory without the Web/computer alternative to support it.

Most learners considered the computer/Web technology medium easy to set up and access, and all the learners considered that the phone/WAP technology could be easily accessed, but two needed help to configure their phones (they missed the face-to-face kickoff event that covered this aspect). Some learners experienced a few problems with the computer/Web material due to incompatibility between some of the HTML code and older browser versions. Overall, the computer and phone technology used in the course was both easy to use and helpful in the learning process by the learners. Common comments were:

"Needs to be more compatible with older browsers."

"The help desk was always quick to solve any problems."

About 80 percent of the course was accessible via the phone, and most learners accessed about 40 to 50 percent of the phone-delivered material. About 90 percent of the course was accessible via the computer, and most learners accessed about 70 to 80 percent of the computer-delivered material. There was some redundancy here, with some of the course material being accessed via both delivery methods. Typical comments related to the use of the WAP phone included:

> "It was good to be able to access the course while traveling in a taxi or waiting for a bus."

> "The phone was particularly useful early on to get an overall feel for the course content."

> "WAP was extremely easy and reliable."

The most common reasons given for accessing the course via the computer more than the WAP phone (for the 70 percent of the course that was available by both means) were that the screen was too small, the connection time was too slow, and the material was more text based than the computer version.

Explain exactly how the application is created and then used by the end user. Explain what software or programming language is used, who is on the team that creates this, and how the user gets it and manipulates it on his or her device. The course was coded using WML [wireless markup language] and resided on an ICUS server. The project team consisted of two course designers, two IT staff members, and a project manager, although none worked full time on just this project.

On the WAP phone, there is an interface that enables the viewing of content in WML format. This interface, referred to as the WML browser, allows learners to make selections in much the same way as on a computer. When a selection is made, the request is transmitted through the StarHub mobile network to the Gateway, which is hosted by the mobile operator.

From the WAP Gateway, a request is sent to the Web server (where the course content resides) to retrieve the desired content. Upon successful retrieval, the Web server returns the content to the WAP Gateway. At this point, the content is encoded into binary form (ones and zeroes) for transmission through the mobile network. The WAP phone receives and displays on the screen the content that is sent on request. At the time of the course deployment (November–December 2000), the rate of content download content was 14.4 Kbytes per second.

How long does it typically take to design and deploy such an application? Given that a Web version already existed, the design and development work [in WML] was completed by the project team in about six weeks. The deployment was conducted over five weeks, within about a week after completion of alpha testing.

No team members worked 100 percent on this project, however, and the total number of "man-weeks" would have also been about six.

What were the biggest challenges or unexpected hurdles? The biggest challenges (none of them unexpected) were small screens, low screen resolution, no color, slow processing, narrow bandwidth, and limited storage capacities.

We avoided the two big challenges confronting m-learning today—a variety of different operating systems (different devices need different formatting of course material) and a lack of network connectivity standards (no instant global reach as with the Web)—by geographically limiting Phase 1 of the project to Singapore (one telecommunications provider—no network problems) and by ensuring that all participants used Nokia 6210 phones so there would be no configuration or keyboard problems.

The difficulty of connecting the various types of these devices to the same network is a very real limitation. Content conversion software has started to emerge to address the problem of delivering on differently configured handheld digital devices. Ideally, m-learning content should comply with a specified standard and be able to run on any system designed for that standard. Proprietary solutions should be able to use any available content and report back results to any systems that comply with the standard.

Because of these technological limitations, there is likely to be a greater focus on delivering learning in very small chunks. Also, there will be a demand for more personalized learning as people demand e-learning in ways designed not only for their needs but also for the device they are using at any particular time.

It seems likely that m-learning will turn out to be better suited to some forms of e-learning than others. Sales reps in the field are a good example. Language learning, with its heavy use of text and sound, may be another. Also, current WAP is best suited to particular aspects of e-learning courses—for example:

- ❐ Quick reminders and alerts from online coaches (SMS or voice)
- ❐ Communication with peers and coaches
- ❐ Multiple-choice quizzes with immediate feedback
- ❐ Memory joggers and tips of the day
- ❐ Glossary information
- ❐ Browsing e-learning course material
- ❐ Searching for specific information within a topic
- ❐ Visits to WAP sites
- ❐ Course registrations

What are your future plans for mobile devices applications for training or business communications with your employees and customers? Phase 1 of the project was confined to fourteen users in Singapore. It is proposed that in Phase 2, the project will expand its geographical reach to Australia, New Zealand, India, and Malaysia, as well as Singapore. It is proposed that Phase 3 will expand the reach further to include Thailand and the Philippines.

Ultimately, the goal is for the reach to be global. The timing of Phases 2 and 3 will depend on technical feasibility in terms of using multiple mobile phone networks in different countries and the capability of conversion software to modify data on the fly according to the multiple mobile phone/PDA configurations that users will have.

We are interested in the performance of DoCoMo in Japan, which has ushered the world into a new era of communications by switching on the first 3G [third-generation] wireless network, bringing high-speed Internet access and a rich mix of data, video, and CD-quality music to wireless devices. It still has problems to solve, but its phones are stretching the boundaries of existing technology, and it will require the faster data rates of 3G to send high-quality pictures and transmit video suitable for m-learning applications.

One key question is whether people will want to watch video clips on their mobile phones. TV station operator Jupiter Programming in Japan is planning to offer content from some of its channels, including a popular golf station, via the eggy [DoCoMo's name for its digital device]. While sales of conventional pocket TVs have never taken off, the use of video within m-learning applications, for example, may be more appealing.

HOW TO CREATE FILES FOR CELL PHONES

Although a cell phone may look as if it is displaying just an ordinary Web site, content needs to be specifically formatted for particular models of cell phones to accommodate their restricted screen size and memory.

The easiest application beyond mere voice calls for cell phones is the use of e-mail. With most Web-enabled cell phones, the process is easy. Most cell phones have specific function buttons to create and send e-mail. Many, like the Kyocera phone, have a built-in Palm operating system, so the screen uses familiar icons and messages are entered by writing in Graffiti on the touch-sensitive screen.

Creating and displaying Web pages on a cell phone is another matter. There are several standards for communicating with various Web-enabled phone devices:

- ❏ WCA (Web clipping applications), used for Palm-compatible devices, also known as PQA (Palm query applications)
- ❏ Handheld device markup language (HDML) used for Web-enabled cell phones
- ❏ WAP (wireless application protocol), a newer standard for Web-enabled phones that uses WML for rendering content

Because of the limited memory of PDAs and cell phones, the applications are actually built in a subset of HTLM and designed so that the static elements of a page reside on the handheld device, while dynamic content is updated over the Internet. This minimizes the amounts of data that need to be transmitted over the slow cell phone lines.

The biggest challenge in translating a conventional Web site to a handheld computer or cell phone format is rearranging the display to fit the small screen and to be readable in monochrome. A few extra "tags" or codes from HTML need to be added that are specific to each device. Some organizations are beginning to sell translators that allow you to build one Web site that automatically recognizes what type of device is trying to display it and then sends the appropriate code on the fly.

A number of Web sites offer tutorials on WML. The WAP Forum, the industry group that develops standards for WAP phones, has a site with a formal definition document for this code's standards. WML, like HTML, is used for specifying the format of text and graphics and creating links among pages. Web sites for cell phones are created with "cards" and "decks." In the WAP standard, pages are called cards, and a set of cards is called a deck; this is like a set of Web pages being considered a site.

Many of the current limitations of cell phone memory and screen size may soon be overcome by new designs as well as by the increasing integration of Pocket PC devices and cell phones. As Microsoft is expanding its Pocket PC operating system and as devices that run this OS are capturing an increasing share of the market, it will be possible to deliver almost any existing Web or e-mail content on these devices since they run Internet Explorer.

CHECKLIST FOR EVALUATING AND LAUNCHING SMART CELL PHONES

Cellular service and phones are almost ubiquitous. Actually, Europe and Asia have much more advanced and pervasive infrastructures than North America, and this medium is especially suited to developing countries where the requirement to string new cable for conventional connections is expensive and slow.

But before leaping into wireless connectivity, consider these factors:

❐ What cellular providers have service in the areas you want to reach? How strong and reliable are the signals, especially within buildings?

❐ What cell phone standard do the available providers use? Remember that there are different communication standards for cell phones and different devices can use only certain standards.

❏ How does the user call up and create messages? Most cell phones force you to use the number keys to enter data, but this is extremely slow for text.

❏ Can the device store messages? Users may want to save e-mails or download instructions or other text so that they don't have to stay online the entire time.

❏ Why do you need to connect wirelessly instead of doing a conventional dial-up with a modem or using the sync function on a PDA?

❏ How might you use even simple messaging to enhance current blended learning environments?

❏ How much will it cost, including the cost of equipment and cellular service? Remember that service agreements and packages are changing very rapidly.

RESOURCES

www.Allnetdevices.com, for information and newsletters about networking devices

www.anywhereyougo.com, news, product announcements and reviews, and tutorials on how to create applications for wireless devices

www.WAPforum.org, WAP Forum's site with standards for WML

Where Am I?

Using GPS for Performance Improvement

I **drive** a truck for a major grocery chain. I use my StreetPilot to mark the position of each store and then use that information to find the best route from store to store. Another great use is when I have received bad route directions and find myself unable to find a store I have not yet entered into it. I simply pull over, enter the address, and it tells me which way to go and how far. This feature has saved me on several occasions.

No red-blooded trucker will ever admit to being lost. When you travel with a touring company like I do, you will see about 175 different cities a year. Keeping up with the 7,500 or so venues is a bit tricky. Paper maps and word of mouth got us there for years. Four or five years ago, I began to incorporate GPS into my work. My marine experience and the simple mapping programs were enough to provide statistical information and directions to waypoints across the nation. I was ridiculed by other truckers because we all knew where we were, but they were finding the time stats interesting and I was verifying a few speedometers. As the units and software became more sophisticated, the jibing ceased and the curiosity picked up. Now with the StreetPilot utilizing the MapSource software, I don't hear a thing from them, and I notice they all line up behind me to guide them into unfamiliar territory.

These are some quotes from typical workers on the go. Drivers present possibly the user population with the most potential for use of global positioning systems, but GPS systems can be used beyond replacing paper maps.

DESCRIPTION OF THE TECHNOLOGY

GPS stands for *global positioning system,* and it is likely that you have used one or at least seen one in a car advertisement. This is the technology that displays where you are on a map as you drive, gives you directions to a location that you select, and is integral to some of the cellular car safety systems like OnStar.

So how does a GPS system work?

The GPS unit does not send out radio signals; it only receives them from navigation satellites in orbit about 12,000 miles above the surface of the earth. These GSP satellites are owned and controlled by the U.S. Department of Defense, which has the prerogative to degrade the accuracy for purposes of national defense. This is done by what is called "selective availability," commonly known as SA. When you turn on your GPS, it starts picking up signals from the satellites, beginning with the strongest signal. Each satellite "knows" where the other satellites are. The GPS system then calculates its distance from each of the satellites to itself. For a good fix, there should be four satellites within a line of sight located around the horizon. GPS systems are accurate within about 10 feet.

The most common uses of GPS systems relate to direction finding in cars, but the applications go beyond this. For workers who spend a lot of time driving in unfamiliar territory (such as sales reps, field technicians, delivery drivers, and home health care providers), this technology can be a huge boost to performance. The GPS system in the car displays the car's location on a map and can provide directions by way of a visual display or speech-synthesized commands. Many organizations are also using GPS systems to track vehicles for dispatching purposes; the closest vehicle to the next job site can be easily routed by a dispatcher who can visually see the location of all available vehicles. GPS systems can also provide monitoring so that a company can track exactly where a driver goes and how long is spent there. For safety purposes, a GPS system can automatically call an ambulance or tow truck when a button is pressed or an alarm or airbag is activated.

Specialized GPS systems can be integrated into other computer and monitoring systems, as we will see, and they are also being produced in versions that can be plugged into a PDA or worn on your wrist.

FORM FACTORS FOR GPS SYSTEMS

Many GPS systems are designed to be mounted in a car or boat; they are used heavily by vacation travelers, hunters, and professional and pleasure boaters. Typical of this kind of system is the Garmin system (see Figure 7.1).

Figure 7.1 A vehicle GPS system. (Courtesy Garmin)

GPS systems can now be bought as add-ons to PDAs (see Figure 7.2). One example is the Geode, which combines Internet information with a GPS that can give you context-based information based on where you are located. The software enables users to browse information linked to interactive maps and interactive travel guides. Users can personalize their map views and search for specific types of places, and then the device shows them where they are on a moving map, provides navigation assistance, and helps them bookmark their favorite places to share with other users.

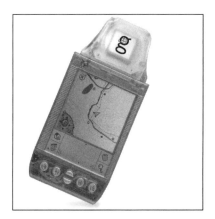

Figure 7.2 Visor with GPS module installed. (Courtesy Handspring)

Even more portable is a wristwatch design by Casio (see Figure 7.3). The watch GPS has a special PC linking program that makes it possible to connect a cable that links the watch to a computer for data exchange. This enables you to download maps and routes into your watch GPS.

The U.S. Federal Communications Commission mandated that starting in October 2001, all cell phones be equipped with GPS systems so that people dialing the emergency 911 number can automatically be located. FCC officials said GPS-equipped handsets will help authorities get to the scene

Figure 7.3 Wristwatch GPS. (Courtesy Casio)

of emergencies faster by tracing the source of 911 calls from mobile phones. This technology could also have other commercial uses, like providing directions to drivers or access to local Yellow Pages.

Up Close

Interview with
Scott Shields Sr., Surveyor,
Phelps Dodge, Morenci, Arizona

GPS systems go beyond the typical way-finding uses. As the next interview proves, they are flexible performance-improvement tools for many applications.

Briefly describe what device you are using and what the applications consist of. Surveyors have used GPS for precise positioning applications at Phelps Dodge [PD] since 1995. At PD, GPS data and navigation applications consist of material and vehicle tracking, surface-to-surface volume calculations, elevation control, machine navigation, road design, and road placement. GPS also provides precise surveying for geologic mapping and mineral exploration. P&H electric mining shovels and Caterpillar track-type tractors use CAES [computer-aided earth-moving system] for various applications. Large electric rotary drills use the Aquila Drill System, and all haul trucks use a modular mining system GPS [see Figure 7.4].

Figure 7.4 GPS system for mining.

What got you started in using the mobile device or devices? GPS was introduced at PD in surveying. Surveyors use GPS as a way to process location data into information for the field supervisor and engineer quickly and efficiently. Location of points, stakeout, volume calculations, and elevation control are the primary uses. As GPS has decreased the survey time and personnel needs, it has given PD surveyors the opportunity to expand their technical expertise to include many more engineering responsibilities. Project development, cost analysis, and civil designs are some of these new responsibilities that surveyors undertake. The efficiency and possible applications of GPS were realized by visionary leadership, and various vendors developed new software and system applications. Caterpillar developed CAES for implementation on mining equipment. Shovels and track-type tractors were first on the list to be installed with GPS units for engineered plan designs.

Explain how the application is used. In 1997, GPS was installed on an electric shovel. P&H mining shovels at PD use CAES for material identification, elevation control, dispatch, and digging boundaries. The highly visible and color display screen is used to show ore polygons, power lines, miscellaneous obstacles, mining limits, and bucket positions. The use of GPS has assisted the development of ore tracking and payload placement. PD has the ability to determine what type of material is being loaded at any given time within the mine boundaries. Each shovel has the capability to mine between 50 and 100 tons of material daily. With this type of earthwork being done, GPS allows for volume-to-volume calculations to calculate accurately how much material is mined and precisely where it was mined. From geologists and mine planners to shift supervisors and shovel operators, every employee now has the ability to see where production data are derived from.

At approximately the same time, the haul trucks were outfitted with a modular mine systems GPS to track haulage routes, destinations, and travel times more accurately. Velocity reports show detailed color-coded speeds to help identify problems within the traffic flow. Our haul truck operators can store points on the fly to identify any problem spots in the field so surveyors can correct or reengineer if necessary. Problem areas are redesigned for proper super, cross slope, and grade to increase truck speeds and operator safety. This type of interactive roadway development provides substantial benefits to the operation. Both operator safety and haulage times profit from maximum utilization and efficiency of mass haul road construction. Road segments are now built with adequate drainage and are designed to match the visibility and handling characteristics of vehicles that weigh more than 300 tons. In addition, the equipment used to build these roadways is more effective in its daily tasks.

The CAES systems were installed on track-type tractors or bulldozers to give the operator real-time feedback on attaining an appropriate design without a surveyor being present. PD uses track-type bulldozers in three main areas.

First, road maintenance dozers are used for mass haul road and project construction. Ramps can include crowns and banking to help keep proper drainage, preserve loads in trucks, and maintain safe but efficient speeds on corners. Design limits can be displayed with text to help give operators direction. It is imperative that roads and ramps be kept smooth to optimize haulage times and decrease equipment wear.

Second, leach stockpile dozers are used to maintain and build new ore stockpiles for material placement. It is crucial to the operation to have accurate volume calculations and precise grade control in these areas. The development of visual sections and stages provides the operator with instructions twenty-four hours a day.

Finally, drilling and blasting is an important front-end component of the mining process. The material must be fractured correctly to mine and haul it efficiently and economically. Fragmentation, or drilling and blasting, dozers use GPS for a number of processes in hard rock mining. The most important of these is the placement of safety berms after a shot. The berm is not only to serve as a safety factor, but also to mark the location that the next drill pattern starts. In addition, the dozers clear and level areas to minimize wear and tear on drills.

In 1998, the first drill was outfitted with the Aquila GPS system. Prior to this installation, pattern layout was the responsibility of one drill supervisor. He laid out patterns for 17 drills and kept the proper amount of broken reserves. The installation of the first Aquila Drill System reduced the number of drill stakes used, reduced pattern layout time, and introduced precise drill navigation.

Realizing that any improvements made in this stage of the mining process could be applied to all the downhill processes, PD changed the way it approached drilling and blasting.

PD surveyors took the task of becoming pattern layout and design engineers. The survey department was challenged with learning new skills and developing open lines of communications with drill supervisors, mechanics, and mine planners. The surveyors' responsibilities now included the precise design planning of drill patterns and the follow-through of making sure the drill operators drilled the pattern as designed. The real value to the survey department was the ability to design and send patterns to GPS-equipped drills and send the pattern to the drill using digital radios. The surveyor does not have to go into the field except to update maps for pattern design. Drillers now have the ability to minimize idle time due to their ability to complete a drill plan and move to the next job progression with centimeter-level accuracy and not have to wait for someone to place new stakes in the field. In addition, supervisors, drillers, and surveyors can now download production information and coordinate values from remote locations.

Recently, the drill navigation systems have proven valu-able to more than just PD's engineering departments. The Aquila systems are also a productivity and efficien-cy monitoring system. The information that engineering uses is primarily the coordinate values. The system is programmed to automatically download diagnostic information from the drills and automatically upload into a series of databases (Access and SQL). We can monitor GPS coverage and availability, drill productivi-ty, and operator accuracy and efficiency and track con-sumables such as drill bits and steel stabilizers.

Blastability index [BI] information is also gained from the drills. The BI is a rock type or rock hardness indica-tor derived directly from operating characteristics of each hole drilled. Tests have proven a correlation of geo-logic structures mapped by geologists and the BI data gathered from the Aquila Drill system database. Once the information, which is measured in 1-inch increments in 62-foot holes, is analyzed by blasting engineers, the hardness boundaries can be mapped and analyzed for fragmentation performance. Positive results are dupli-cated in areas of matching geologic characteristics.

We have come a long way from in-the-field paper nap-kin design and hood-top directions. In fact, armed with information, we are affecting every facet of the mine planning. Our blast engineers can determine the need for more or less equipment in certain zones and plan to change the geometry of the pattern designs and the amount of blasting agent needed to achieve the desired fragmentation. Surveyors, blast engineers, maintenance departments, and geologists make more informed deci-sions than ever before.

What have been the business or productivity results? Using the GPS navigation system instead of conventional surveying methods saves an enormous amount of survey time on every task—about 3,900 hours or $70,000 in survey time annually. Supply savings were estimated at $8,500 for stockpiles, ramps, and various tasks. Blastline layout projected savings near $750,000 by eliminating rework. Other rework savings on stockpiles and shovel pits are estimated at $590,000. Stockpile recovery loss equated to approximately $60,000. There are also projected savings for equipment wear, but the numbers are difficult to quantify.

Three factors are considered when optimizing the placement of GPS navigation units: safety, survey time, and dollar value. These factors are ranked by application from one to five in order of importance or relevance, where 1 is the best or highest ranking:

Application	Safety	Time	Cost Savings
Ramps and roads	1	3	2 ($690,000)
Special projects	3	4	4 ($33,000)
Stockpiles	1	2	3 ($220,000)
Property boundaries	—	5	5 ($1,500)
Blast lines and drill clean-up	—	1	1 ($790,000)

Ramps, roads, and stockpiles were all given the same safety rank due to the proximity of personnel to heavy machinery. The greatest amount of time is saved on blast lines and drill areas, which also have the greatest cost saving.

The savings to date have been accrued from reduction in rework, supplies, surveyor time, and timeliness of project completion. Over the past year, GPS navigation systems have been on track-dozers throughout the PD mine. Two units are used by drilling and blasting, one by leaching and stockpiling, and three by road maintenance to get a representative sample of the savings that a GPS navigation unit provides. Drilling and blasting used the track-dozers 50 percent of the time on blast lines, 40 percent of the time establishing drill pads, and the remaining 10 percent trenching final crest lines for shovels. Leaching and stockpiling used their unit 65 percent of the time for building stockpiles and 5 percent of the time creating ramps for new lifts. The remaining 30 percent of the time the GPS was unused. Road maintenance used its navigation systems 40 percent of the time for making new roads and ramps. Maintaining existing haul roads and ramps made up 50 percent of the time, and the remaining 10 percent was used for leveling shovel pits. The total savings amounted to $0.95 million during the past year on these six track-dozer GPS navigation systems, which equates to a payback of five months.

Explain exactly how the application is created and then used by the end user. Explain what software or programming language is used, the team that created this, and how the user gets it and manipulates it on his or her device. The CAES uses onboard computers for mining machines, software, GPS, and data radios and receivers to greatly reduce the need for conventional surveying [see Figures 7.5 and 7.6]. First, mine plans are generated by common computer-aided design software. The plans are then translated into a format used by the CAES on-board system and communicated directly to the machine using a high-speed radio

system developed jointly by Trimble Navigation and
Caterpillar. This information is in the form of a three-
dimensional digital terrain model. An onboard color
monitor mounted in the machine cab displays the virtual site plan for the operator. As the machine works, terrain updates are performed continuously using GPS
technology. This information is then updated on the
operator's display and simultaneously transmitted back
to the office where a manager feeds the data to the
CAES office. The mine manager or engineer can view
several machines working at the same time. Up-to-the-
minute data can then be exported to the original planning software for any additional design work or plan
changes.

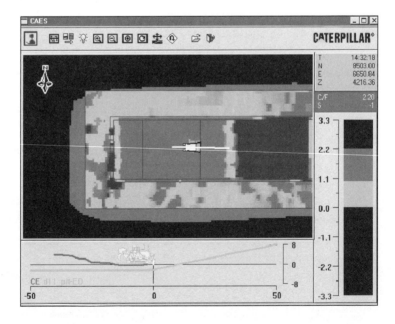

Figure 7.5 CAES operator screen.

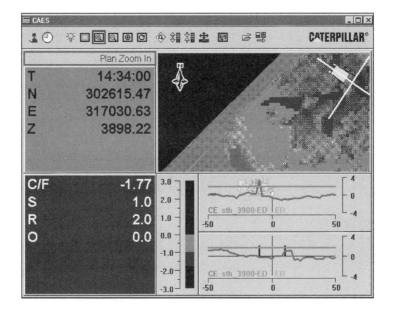

Figure 7.6 CAES operator screen.

How long does it typically take to design and deploy such an application? Caterpillar did the original development of the CAES system. Once a demo model was created, PD was used as a beta test site for approximately one year to further the development of CAES before open market introduction.

As for the end user, that is, PD, once the mine plan has been designed, it is quickly transmitted via the radio network right to the machine. The machine position information is updated in real time and simultaneously sent back to the mine office for analysis and planning. New applications are continuously developed for CAES and the operators that use it.

What were the biggest challenges or unexpected hurdles? The biggest challenge affecting the implementation of any new technology is to gain the acceptance of the workers. Many of the operators employed have years of experience and at times are uncertain of new technologies and their reason for implementation. It is extremely important to have acceptance and participation of these employees to maximize the use of such technologies. Once operators understand the technology is a tool to aid in their production efforts, they will expand on the development of the tool to its maximum potential. A hurdle in the development of GPS technologies is the development of seamless radio networks. At PD, we have two separate GPS base stations to supply ample radio communications for the amount of personnel and equipment requiring GPS correctional data. There are over 3,000 handheld radios on site, so creating room for extra lines of communications was a key to the success of GPS implementation. PD has ten highly skilled and trained technicians at the Morenci site to ensure minimal down time of all RF solutions.

What are your future plans for mobile device applications for training or business communications with your employees, students, and customers? Advanced communication infrastructures will be critical in the development of intelligent mining systems. Bandwidth requirements will continue to challenge vendors and users to move diagnostics, logistics support, and control systems in an ever-changing mining environment. To look to the future, one would have to look at systems similar to advanced combat systems. It is a wireless world, and industry will have to learn to embrace these visions to revolutionize mining. Technical expertise in these areas will be critical to the realizations of goals. Turnkey solutions provided by vendors that do not understand the arduous conditions faced in a mining environment will be continuously challenged to provide tomorrow's technology today. We plan on pushing our vendors to meet and exceed the standards necessary for the development of intelligent mining equipment, enhancing safety and production.

What advice would you give to fellow training, business performance, and communications professionals with regard to getting into the use of mobile devices? It is critical to the evolution of new technology in the end-user arena to constantly provide technical training to operators. Although engineering makes use of the data at PD, it is the operators' experience and input that truly advance technology and the applications in which they are used. It is important to request support services from dealers of mobile technologies to minimize downtime due to faulty hardware or software. If the technologies are used as designed, benefits will be realized only for the current applications. Constantly visualize new applications for technology and develop data pertinent to your operation. Don't be afraid to ask what you can do to make processes better.

GPS SYSTEMS FOR DRIVER PERFORMANCE IMPROVEMENT

An obvious application for GPS systems is for drivers: couriers, delivery personnel, taxi and limousine drivers, and emergency vehicle operators. Not only can GPS systems give them directions, but these systems can also be used to track a fleet at a main office or dispatch center. GPS systems can be integrated with other software that can encompass fleet management and routing, as well as performance tracking.

UP CLOSE

Interview with
Bill Kimler, Distribution Systems Manager,
Maines Paper & Food Service,
Binghamton, New York

One company using an innovative suite of GPS and handheld computer tools is Maines Paper & Food Service in upstate New York.

Explain how GPS systems are used to monitor and improve the productivity of drivers. Most large transportation companies make use of onboard computer systems that interface directly with the tractor engines not only to provide physical information such as miles traveled and fuel consumed but also to make legal recordings of drivers' activities to ensure compliance with Department of Transportation regulations. There is also much useful information that can be gleaned from these systems to monitor driver productivity, alert management to safety issues (such as frequent speeding or sudden braking), and provide a real-time monitoring system.

Maines Paper & Food Service installed the Xata On-Board Computer Systems [*www.xata.com*] in all five of its distribution centers in the Northeast. The implementation began in October 2000 and was completed in the last distribution center by November 2001. Within each truck, a number of pieces of hardware can be found.

The Xata driver computer is a touch-screen interface

that provides a simple text interface with which the driver can record delivery and duty information [see Figure 7.7]. It provides constant information as to driving speed and expected arrival times for deliveries. It also allows the driver to send and receive text messages with dispatch clerks back at the office. This type of real-time information exchange has allowed us to communicate immediately with the drivers, and vice versa, allowing us to take advantage of backhaul (money-making) opportunities and to cut down on customer involvement, such as calling each customer on a particular route looking for a driver, which not only inconveniences the customer but could also cause unnecessary worry.

Figure 7.7 Driver computer.

The driver computer is on the low end of computing power and was designed prior to the widespread use of GPS and communication. To protect the investment that many companies had already made in these driver computers, Xata created MAS [mobile application server], which is a literal black-box add-on that contains more computing power used specifically for GPS capture and interpretation and for real-time communications, whether it be through a cellular network or a satellite network [see Figure 7.8]. Its GPS capabilities can detect state-line crossings automatically, which used to be a driver-entry process, and also associate GPS coordinates with nearest cities and states. The MAS system can also be configured to send information about the route automatically, without any driver input. This allows our dispatch clerks to be able to monitor the progress of all routes currently dispatched—much like NASA mission control!

Figure 7.8 Mobile application server.

The Mobitex antenna assists with the wireless communications between the vehicle and the office [see Figure 7.9]. It works through an exchange of data over a cellular network (through Cingular Interactive) in much the same way that a digital cell phone works. The GPS antenna provides the interface between the signals made freely available from U.S. government satellites and the vehicle. Every 5 seconds, the antenna reads the coordinates from the satellite and transmits it to the MAS device for storage and interpretation.

Figure 7.9 Mobitex and GPS antennas.

Each driver is issued a driver Xata key, which is really a memory chip used for batch transfer of information from the vehicle back to a fixed station in the office [see Figure 7.10]. In order to cut down on communication costs, any information that is not of a real-time, urgent nature is stored on the key and transferred at the end of the trip for further processing. This key maintains seven days' worth of electronic logs that contain all of the required DOT information that can be recalled from the driver computer at any DOT checkpoint.

Figure 7.10 Driver key.

What results have you seen from your new GPS system so far? The results that we've seen are more qualitative in nature than they are quantitative. GPS has not led to an increase in sales or driver productivity.

However, we now have the ability to report back to ourselves and to our customers accurate on-time delivery information. In the past, when a driver recorded that he was at Stop A at a certain time, we were relying on the honesty of the driver. He could have easily been somewhere down the road when recording the delivery. GPS keeps the drivers honest; when he records a stop, our software compares the GPS coordinates of that stop with the known coordinates of the customer to whom he is supposed to be delivering.

In conjunction with the communications equipment, real-time tracking of our trips is possible. Our clerks are now reacting to trips that fall behind schedule prior to the customers' knowing about it. Instead of our customers' informing us that their deliveries are late, we are able to notify them ahead of time, and that has made all the difference in customer satisfaction. A customer tends not to mind a late delivery as much if he or she is given adequate notification.

Finally, the GPS data collected have been slowly incorporated into our routing software. Typical routing software comes with address-matching algorithms that geocode a new location based on its shipping address. This address matching, however, can be highly inaccurate, sometimes placing the location in the center of a ZIP code region. This has created difficulty in planning the routes. If the locations are not accurately positioned, the routes will not be accurately created. The GPS data, however, change all that. We are getting precise coordinates back from the trucks that are actually at the sites. We hope to see significant improvement in the accuracy of our plans in the coming months.

What recommendations would you give another company that wanted to use similar GPS systems for its drivers? Make sure that the intangible benefits gained from these devices are worth the cost. By itself, GPS is not very useful. In conjunction with communications, integrated software to interpret the data, and the personnel in place to monitor and make decisions based on the received information, GPS then becomes more than just a tech toy.

HOW TO USE GPS DEVICES

GPS devices differ in terms of their end-user functionality, but all of them have the same basic requirements. They function by receiving signals from special navigation satellites, and the units figure out their location by triangulation. To triangulate, a GPS receiver measures distance using the travel time of radio signals to the GPS receiver and compares the travel times among at least three satellites.

GPS can be used for several applications:

Location. Using a GPS and maps that are either stored on the unit or downloaded from the Internet or CD-ROMs, a GPS can display position graphically and in precise terms using longitude and latitude, with an accuracy of a few feet.

Navigation. A GPS system with mapping and routing software can aid drivers, pilots, and boat captains in finding the most expedient route from one place to another. For example, John McCarthy, a training officer for Corporate Jet's Air Medical Services Division, praises the use of GPS navigation for the University of Wisconsin Hospital and Clinics. The system allows pilots to check their flight accuracy and conditions for approach continuously; they can automatically sequence up to forty flight plans with forty waypoints each, show the nearest airport, plan vertical descents, and display minimum safe altitudes.

Tracking. GPS systems can monitor the movement of people and things. Many trucking and public safety applications use this functionality to display the location of vehicles continuously so that they can be dispatched more efficiently. Small GPS systems can now track people as well as equipment and can be used for asset management. They can precisely determine where a given piece of equipment is located.

Mapping. Using the precise data on location, organizations can more efficiently map areas. For instance, utility companies can precisely and quickly map out water and sewer lines, and large plant facilities can more easily develop precise maps of their buildings, water and electrical services, and features of the landscape.

Timing. GPS satellites bring precise timing to the world because they all use precise atomic clocks; therefore, other devices can be set to their accurate times. One investment banking firm uses GPS to guarantee that its transactions are recorded simultaneously at all offices around the world. A major Pacific Northwest utility company makes sure that its power is distributed at just the right time along its 14,797 miles of transmission lines using GPS receivers.

Using GPS systems generally requires two components:

1. Ensuring that the device can "see" or receive signals from at least three satellites

2. Loading and using maps associated with the locations where the system will be used

Most GPS systems are "bundled" with software, specifically mapping software. More sophisticated and integrated systems also include routing software, asset management databases, and hardware and software that can control other devices such as factory automation, material handling, or construction equipment. Obviously, the operation of these systems is unique to the application.

☐ CHECKLIST FOR EVALUATING AND LAUNCHING GPS SYSTEMS

☐ What's your overall use of GPS? Typical applications for performance improvement include:

☐ Helping mobile workers find the best directions to new destinations

☐ Tracking mobile workers and equipment for performance monitoring, for efficiency in dispatching, and for improving the safety of the workers

☐ Asset management in terms of being able to locate key pieces of equipment

☐ Being able to time and coordinate events precisely

☐ Determine the type of GPS system you need. Do you want something permanently installed in a vehicle or a portable system? Do you want a stand-alone unit or something that snaps into a PDA?

☐ Does the GPS system come with maps built in, or do they have to be downloaded? How much memory does the GPS system have to store maps? Will enough maps be able to be stored between downloading if the users frequently go to different locations?

☐ Make sure that the GPS system will be able to "see" and receive satellite data from the desired locations. It is often difficult or impossible to use these within buildings or under obstacles such as bridges and tunnels.

☐ Ensure that the users know how to use the GPS system and are comfortable with being monitored.

❐ Make sure that you have communicated how and when the data will be used to take care of ethical as well as legal issues regarding privacy.

RESOURCES

www.garmin.com, the world's largest manufacturer of GPS systems

www.trimble.com/gps/index.html, a good tutorial on GPS systems

www.palmgear.com, hardware and software for Palm-compatible computers

Dick Tracy Had the Right Stuff

Wearable Devices

and Beyond

As I write this chapter, an interesting conference is going on: tech-u-wear 2001 in New York City. This is where display manufacturers, wireless technology companies, chip manufacturers, battery producers, "smart fabric" makers, and speech recognition companies are meeting to forge the future of the industry and make crucial strategic partnerships. An interesting note appears on the conference Web site about a last-minute program addition.

Alex Lightman, the CEO of Charmed Technologies, is presenting a summary of how wearable and pervasive computing devices may be used for security, surveillance and disaster relief operations—a powerful but sad example of how the events of September 11, 2001, have changed so much of the focus of society and new technologies.

The previous chapters in this book provided a tour of wonderful new devices and the applications that you can employ today to improve learning and performance in organizations. But we are seeing only the beginning of this mobile computing environment. Here is a peek at what is next:

- ❏ Cheap, fast, third-generation cell phone access, which makes wireless computing nearly ubiquitous

- ❏ Smart wallets that allow people to "beam" funds from their bank accounts instead of handling cash or credit cards

- ❏ Place-sensitive devices, which alert consumers as to which nearby entertainment, food, and products are on their profile of favorites; electronic coupons stored in a cell phone or PDA allow for instant rebates and discounts

- ❏ Wearable computers, which will have integrated cell phone and voice recognition capabilities

- ❏ Training and information available in small bytes on demand and tailored not only to the user's input but based on the user's actual behaviors and location

Gartner Research has predicted an integrated set of enablers that it says will bring about the kind of major discontinuities that propel profound changes in the way that business-to-business and business-to-consumer interactions occur (see Figure 8.1). These marketing innovations will drive widespread consumer purchases of new devices that will provide the necessary installed base for corporate training and performance improvement interventions to come along easily and inexpensively.

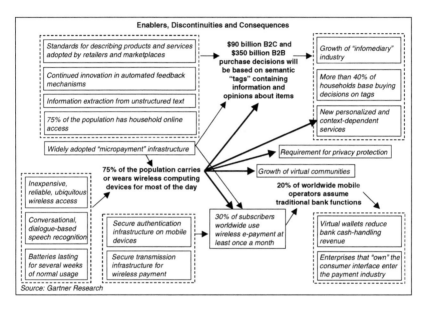

Figure 8.1 Enablers of mobile communications infrastructure. (Courtesy Gartner Research, J. Fenn, A. Linden, "Hottest of the Hot Discontinuities of the Next Decade," April 2001)

WEARABLE COMPUTERS

Dick Tracy paved the way decades ago: He wore a watch that allowed him to communicate with his fellow crime fighters. That kind of device—and more—is available now. Computers are becoming smaller, and it is possible to buy a PDA for your wrist, like the model by Casio shown in Figure 8.2.

Although it is obviously difficult to get much computer power or display space on something small enough to wear on a wrist, other form factors for wearable computers are available, and new systems are being developed. Both MIT and Georgia Tech University have significant ongoing research projects relating to wearable computers.

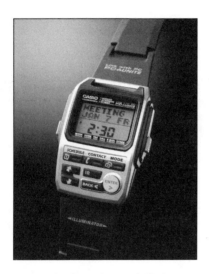

Figure 8.2 Casio wristwatch PDA.

While the prototypes in Figures 8.3 and 8.4 look unattractive and improbable, there are much more attractive and functional systems in use right now. The U.S. military has been using hands-free wearable computers for some time now to offer training and technical manuals for military equipment use and repair. Similar systems are now being made available to the general public.

For example, BOC Gases sells nitrogen, oxygen, and carbon dioxide to more than ten thousand customers who use the products to control temperature during their manufacturing processes. BOC has launched an independent company, Thinkage, with service technicians who use wearable computers with wrist-mounted keyboards and head-mounted displays and can move among buildings and locations to solve line problems and fix equipment (see Figure 8.5). According to Mark Grace, president of Thinkage and developer of Thinkage's Think Gate computerized monitoring and performance support system, "the plants using this system are achieving single- and double-digit increases in productivity." Thinkage installs sensors and video screens at manufacturing cells. Real-time feedback on line activities is monitored with sensors placed at critical change points in the line. A local network receives and manages the real-time data. The wearable computers provide continual visual feedback from line functions directly at each cell. These mobile technicians can be at the cell site to observe the problem and help resolve it, with their hands free to do the work. Real-time equipment repair is supported by Thinkage's online technical information system, Customer Equipment and Service Data (CESD). Using CESD, a technician can find and view a user guide, repair manual, or other pertinent operational information on various types of process.

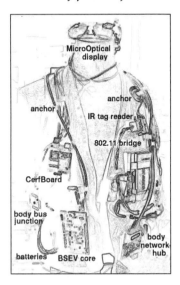

Figure 8.3 MIT wearable prototype diagram. (Courtesy MIT Media Lab)

Figure 8.4 MIT prototype wearable computer. (Courtesy MIT Media Lab)

Figure 8.5 A BOC technician using a wearable computer. (Courtesy Xybernaut Corporation)

UP CLOSE

Interview with
Jennifer Ockerman, Research Engineer,
Georgia Tech Research Institute, Atlanta, Georgia

As performance improvement professionals look for opportunities to deploy job aids and electronic performance support systems, research from Georgia Tech provides useful inspiration.

Briefly describe what device you are using and what the applications consist of. Our research explores the issues associated with creating an electronic performance support system [EPSS] for a mobile industrial workforce. The FAST [factory automation support technology] system has two primary purposes: (1) to improve human performance in manufacturing systems and (2) to link mobile personnel with plantwide databases and experts in real time. Human performance is supported through the timely presentation of technical information or advice necessary to operate, adjust, or repair advanced complex automation. Mobile personnel are able to continuously update and retrieve information from a central database while roaming throughout a large space. They also can make video connections with experts to get help with their current tasks.

The FAST hardware is a wearable, multimedia-capable, voice-activated computer system [see Figure 8.6]. The first component is a head-mounted display, which allows the user to interact with the environment while viewing text, drawings, animations, and videos that are pertinent to what the user is doing. The position in space of the computer image can be adjusted by the user for maximum viewing comfort. The display fits comfortably over glasses and can be tilted up out of the way when it is not needed. Next, the system includes a miniature microphone and earphone headset that provides audio information to the user and accepts voice input from the user. The audio information can include explanatory narrations, audio prompts or reminders, alarm signals, or diagnostic cues. Voice activation allows users to keep their hands free for job-related tasks while interacting with the EPSS. For noisy industrial environments, a headset with a noise-canceling microphone and stereo earphones is used. The sound-muffling earphones protect the user's hearing, and the noise-canceling microphone allows the user to maintain audio communication with the computer. This technology has been proven effective in environments where the ambient noise level is above 90 decibels.

A third component is a small video camera attached to the front of the headset. The camera enables the user to transmit his or her view of the workplace to a distant site to aid in remote collaboration. The camera may also be removed and used as a handheld camera to access hard-to-see places. The fourth component is a wireless communication device that sends and receives up-to-date information to and from a plant computer system. A range of 600 feet between stations is feasible in an open area when commercially available wireless local area adapters are used. By connecting to a shared database, the plant management can access real-time information, such as quality assurance data, as it is gathered by mobile workers. Also, the mobile user can access additional information that is not stored on the wearable computer or connect with remote sites via the Internet.

Figure 8.6 Head-mounted visual and audio devices.

The ultraportable, wearable computer is the fifth component [see Figure 8.7]. The computer is worn on a belt at the waist, allowing the user to enter and receive information while moving throughout a plant. In addition to voice activation, the wearable computer is equipped with a small touch pad to move the display cursor and select objects on the display. This device is included as a backup to the voice control. The current wearable computer we are using includes a 486 75 MHz Intel processor, 24 MB of RAM, a 340 MB hard disk, a high resolution display controller, serial and parallel ports, a mouse port, 16-bit audio, and three additional PCMCIA (PC card) expansion slots. The current generation of the wearable computer weighs approximately 3 pounds, plus batteries. The final component is a battery pack to supply power to all the components. The battery is worn on the belt around the waist or within the same container as the computer.

Figure 8.7 Mobile tablet computers allow data collection in the field.

Most recently, we have focused on using mobile devices in the poultry industry to aid in the collection of quality data. For this project, we have used a Via wearable computer with a hand-held display with an option of voice or pen input [selection of links in a Web page is the method of interacting whether using voice or pen]. This year we are also evaluating the use of Compaq iPaqs with a wireless connection. Currently, we are using pen input but will look at voice input as soon as that becomes available.

What got you started in using the mobile device or devices? We needed a way to allow the inspectors who move throughout a poultry plant to collect quality data and have those data in real time for the plant managers. The only way to do this in the poultry plant was with wireless, mobile devices. It had been discovered in the past that having computers available on the plant floor was not feasible due to the rigorous cleaning that is done in poultry processing plants.

Explain how the application is used. Who are the users, and what is the setting? The application is designed to be used by the poultry plant inspectors, their supervisors, and their managers. The entire system allows for the generation of data collection procedures, the collection of data, the design of data dissemination procedures and reports, and the dissemination of the data to appropriate personnel both within and outside the poultry processing facility. The setting is a poultry processing facility, which is large, noisy, damp, and messy.

What have been the business or productivity results? One short initial test showed that the inspector could collect the required data in half the amount of time previously required with paper. However, one of our goals this fiscal year is to evaluate the business case of using this type of system for quality data collection, so we have no firm results at this point.

Explain exactly how the application is created and then used by the end user. Explain what software or programming language is used, who is on the team that created this, and how the user gets it and manipulates it on his or her device. We use a browser as the interface to the system and all the programs are asp pages with vbscript; these are standard programming languages. Programmers within our institute have designed software so that the quality assurance managers can design new data collection procedures that are automatically generated in a format that guides the inspectors through the collection of quality data.

What are your future plans for mobile devices applications for training or business communications with your employees, students, and customers? We plan to continue with the current project and also look into tying the data that we have humans collecting with data that can be collected automatically by sensors. We also hope to get back to more of a training angle with the maintenance of equipment and automation in poultry plants.

THE INTELLIGENT ENVIRONMENT

The idea of pervasive computing is not limited to wireless devices and wearable computers; another trend in information and performance improvement is the creation of intelligent environments. I have a film from the 1970s that I sometimes show students that depicts a young family in about the year 2000. They wear shiny jumpsuits and have a totally wired and automated home. It starts out with birds singing and the drapes in the master bedroom automatically opening, the stove turning on to make coffee, and envelopes of mail and newspapers pouring in from a slot that was being filled up by a printer. Well, many of us have automatic coffeemakers, and we do get e-mail (but not in envelopes!). The environment was also scanned by various sensors, and the vital health statistics of each family member were fed into a home computer with a big screen. The kids went to school, and the parents worked and ordered clothes and garden supplies via this same strange big screen with a keyboard.

Smart homes have been prototyped many times, and in almost all cases, new devices for automating typical residential activities have not worked or been accepted well. However, there may be forthcoming changes in society, the economy, and the workplace that will make these applications more attractive. While it is possible to embed information in devices that people carry around or wear, it may be more feasible in some cases to have the devices embedded in the environment. For example, if an organization wants to create a high-performance conference room, smart devices can be embedded to sense activities, provide intelligent advice and tailored information, and offer specialized tools for collaboration and decision support. In a factory environment, sensors can monitor key environmental and production variables and provide performance support to those in the area.

The potential for smart environments is being explored by the Smart Medical Home project research laboratory that simulates the networked home environment. This five-room "house," located within the University of Rochester Medical Center, is outfitted with infrared sensors, computers, biosensors, and video cameras for use by research teams to work with research subjects as they test concepts and prototype products (see Figure 8.8). These research teams address the technical, informational, and human issues that will form the basis for affordable health care products that can be easily used by people with varying abilities. The overall goal is to develop pervasive "whole home" systems so all technologies are integrated and work seamlessly.

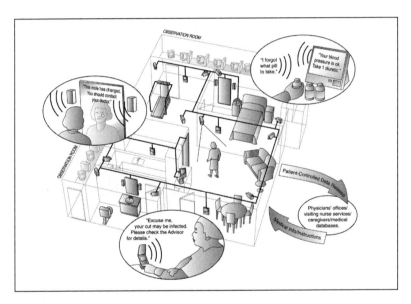

Figure 8.8 Prototype smart home at the University of Rochester Medical School.

Two of the prototype technologies include a smart mirror that detects changes in a person's mole over time and a bandage that detects infection in a wound (see Figure 8.9). These technologies could be adapted to work settings to monitor health, ergonomics, environment, and status of tools and machinery.

Figure 8.9 Biometric devices can provide blood pressure readings and detect infections in wounds.

☐ CHECKLIST FOR ADOPTING PERVASIVE COMPUTING

We have clearly not seen the ultimate in pervasive, wearable computing. Scientists are already working on implantable devices, computer "jewelry," and environments that are literally saturated with computing and sensor devices. But how will they affect learning and performance in organizations? There are certainly many critical managerial and ethical concerns:

☐ *Will these devices increase or impede learning?* Although mobile, wearable computers may provide learning on the go, they may also become popular alternatives to learning. It is very tempting to offer performance support devices that work something like a "brain prosthesis" so that, in fact, people do not have to learn to perform their jobs. But will these cyber-coaches replace learning? Will we create a workplace of unquestioning, docile human-robots?

☐ *Will pervasive computing create a hostile work environment?* It is quite tempting to wire people and environments so that managers and coaches know where they are and what they are doing at all times. But is there no privacy in the workplace? Will this kind of technology create a big-brother environment that adds stress and decreases trust? Will this take us back to an even harsher scientific management style after having worked for so many decades to create a more humanistic and empowered philosophy?

❑ *How will these devices affect the health and safety of people?* Wearable devices and environmental scanning systems can clearly promote safety: We can keep out intruders, cast a watchful eye on employees in remote areas, and even monitor vital signs of individuals in their home and workplace. But we do not yet know the effect of close and prolonged exposure to electronic devices and wireless transmissions; the jury is still out on the effects of cell phone and monitor radiation, for example. Will the stress caused by being "always on" and drowned by messages and information counteract any possible performance enhancement that these devices might create?

❑ *Will users resist these new gizmos?* Most educated and employed individuals have become accustomed to—or inured to—the constant flux of technology. But wearable devices are beyond simply a new operating system or word processing application. The devices look odd and may feel uncomfortable. Indeed, one of the biggest obstacles for wearable computers is fashion: They do not complement the clothes that many people wear. Interestingly, a major push now by the manufacturers of wearables is to make them a fashion statement (see Figure 8.10).

And you thought that being a trainer and performance consultant was tough enough already! Now, welcome to the world of fashion and interior design!

Figure 8.10 Wearable computers can be chic. (Courtesy Xybernaut Corporation)

RESOURCES

> *http://wearables.www.media.mit.edu/projects/wearables/*, the Massachusetts Institute for Technology Web site on wearable computing research
>
> *http://mime1.gtri.gatech.edu/tim/default.htm*, the Georgia Tech Web site on intelligent machines
>
> *www.xybernaut.com*, a major vendor of wearable computers
>
> *www.charmed.com*, for the future of fashionable and effective wearables
>
> *www.casio.com*, the producer of watch-style cameras and computing devices

Getting Up to Internet Speed

Managing the New Landscape of Learning and Performance

WE **HAVE** explored some fascinating new devices and explored what the future might hold for mobile devices, training, and performance improvement. But employing these devices is not enough to make the radical change that is required. In order to make use of them, we need to rewire not only our technology but also our approaches to managing training and even managing people.

I want to invite you to join me in staring into my crystal ball and to look at a scenario that is not far off. Then I want us to consider the implications of these technologies for our practice and the quality of personal and work experience for those we serve and for our society.

> It's 7 A.M., and Keri starts the day by retrieving her PDA from its cradle and sipping a hot cup of herbal tea. Keri is a performance and learning specialist for General International Zoomer Merchant Organization (GIZMO), a professional society of professionals in the zoomer industry, a rapidly growing group of manufacturers and sellers of zoomers, which are one-person transportation devices that can fly or drive using solar power. Keri lives on a farm in upstate New York; the rest of the support staff for GIZMO is located across the globe; there is no central office. Keri is responsible for creating training and other performance support tools for GIZMO members. As she takes that first sip of tea out on her back deck, she turns on her PDA and sees a display of new e-mails and news items that have accumulated overnight.
>
> She taps her finger on the message from the association president, Ryan, who is in England. It says that in the think tank he held yesterday via teleconference with some of the industry leaders, they discussed a need to train people in zoomer consumer sales about some of the new solar technologies they will be bringing to market. Keri is about to dictate a response

to Ryan about setting up a conference call when she notices a yellow smiling face next to Ryan's e-mail address, indicating that he is online now. Because she knows with the time difference that he will not be in his office much longer, she gives the voice command "Connect to Ryan," and up on her screen comes an "accepted" message and then Ryan's smiling face. Her PDA has a built-in camera, speaker, and microphone so she can do teleconferencing using her cellular phone connection without leaving the sunshine of her deck.

"Hey Keri—you're starting the day early. How are you?" says Ryan.

"Great, but what are you doing in Italy?" Keri asks. (All PDA and cell phones have built-in GPS systems, so Keri knows immediately where Ryan is located.)

"My partner and I decided to take a long weekend here, knowing I could take care of business from the hotel. So, anyway, in the think tank yesterday, we were commenting on the trouble that sales reps throughout the industry are having in explaining some of the new solar panels. Consumers simply don't understand or trust them, nor do they see the payback in using the more expensive solar panels versus charging batteries with electricity. Do you think we might be able to get some generic training available on our Web site to offer our members?"

Keri thinks over the request and says,

"Sure. I'm sure we can get some industry experts to help us develop some information and post a course to the Web. But I'm not sure it's really best solved by training."

"Tell me more," says Ryan. "Why not training?"

Keri responds, "I'm thinking that perhaps coming up with a job aid that sales reps could use as they work with customers might be more effective and quicker— maybe something that they could share with customers so that the consumers themselves could do the payback analysis and do some what-ifs."

"I like it," says Ryan. "Look, you're the expert. I'll leave it up to you, and besides, I want to get off now and try to catch a boat excursion. Let me know what you come up with."

Keri signs off and takes a walk around her pond to get her creative juices flowing. Back at her desk, she goes online to the GIZMO expert matchmaker site. She puts in a request for subject matter experts who are knowledgeable in solar technologies and successful sales reps who have sold it. Within a few hours, she gets three responses, and while driving to lunch with the graphic designer who is helping her with some projects, she gets a call on her car phone from Luiz in Brazil. Luiz is the top sales rep in Latin America for zoomers, and he offers to share his secrets. Despite the fact that he speaks only Spanish, they can communicate with little trouble since they are using the auto-translate feature of their cell phone service.

Luiz has a spreadsheet that he uses to calculate payback on the solar systems, and he also recommends a colleague in India who is terrific at connecting with customers. Luiz attaches his spreadsheet to an e-mail to Keri, and Keri gets Rama in India to do a little audio role-play with her coworker. The audio file is sent as an MP3 file.

Within a day, Keri is able to put together a sales support package that members can download from the GIZMO Web site. It is done in a format that works on desktop and laptop PCs, smart cell phones, and a whole variety of PDAs. Not only can the payback spreadsheet be used by sales reps, but it can be wirelessly beamed to customers' PDAs and Web phones so that they can use it at home. An announcement about the availability of the new tool is broadcast to all GIZMO members in the sales special interest group, and Keri can see from her Web management tracking system that it was downloaded sixty-six times in the first day.

Does this sound like science fiction? Some of the technologies, like wireless videoconferencing or automatic translation on the fly, are not quite ready for prime time yet, but they are most certainly in the wings. Clearly, new instructional design and project management systems are needed.

ASKING ALL THE WRONG QUESTIONS

How much does an hour of mobile training cost? How much time should instructional designers, programmers, and subject matter experts spend in creating a course? What authoring and record-keeping software do we need to license in order to administer online curricula? Hard questions to answer? Guess what! Don't answer them. They are the wrong questions.

Concepts like "hours" of training, "courses," and "online curricula" are out of sync with mobile learning and performance improvement. They are taking the worst problems of classrooms and schooling and imposing them on a new system that does not have the constraints of time, fixed project time frames and personnel, top-down information, and certification requirements. These traditional mind-sets follow an antiquated university model and are too slow, rigid, and expensive for most situations.

Several clients in the past year have asked me to help them create online courses. They had in mind five- or six-figure budgets and were prepared to wait a half a year. I surprised them by showing them how they could create the foundation for a much more dynamic online learning and performance system in about a day (and for a much lower cost). With the move to mobile learning, small chunks of targeted information, and possibilities for wireless connection, collaboration, and coaching, processes like this are critical to implement. I do it by creating a framework for an intranet site that includes these components:

- Small chunks of instruction (like definitions, illustrations, and short explanations of critical concepts) that can usually be derived from existing documentation or instructional manuals

- Links to other sites that contain relevant articles or case studies (online versions of newspapers, business magazines, or university professors' sites are good places to look)

- Case studies drawn from a few selected content experts or members of the target user population

- Job aids like spreadsheet templates, word processing forms, and checklists

- An "expert of the month" page where people inside and outside the organization can take turns in answering e-mail questions addressed to them

- A threaded discussion group where users can post questions and answers to each other

I generally create most of the Web pages using the built-in editors that come free with my Web browser. If you can use a word processor, you can learn to use these Web page composers in under an hour. Most of my clients already have lots of information stored in word processing files; they can instantaneously be transformed into an HTML (hypertext mark-up language) format for Web pages by using the Save as HTML command available in almost every word processing package. Many times, electronic slide presentations already exist for meetings or classes on a topic. By editing these a bit and using the Save as HTML command, you can export them as a series of Web pages. If they are not self-explanatory, we can get the presenter to record an audio narration or add some slides.

Instead of making sites that are "courses that people take," we develop "systems that collaborators make." We come up with site names like "FAST: Financial Analysis Systems Tools," which suggest information sharing, continuous learning, ongoing documentation of best practices, and quick performance solutions (see Figure 9.1). I have gotten case studies and even short audio scripts to seed the site by e-mailing prospective users. Using a digital camera or asking participants to send in pictures that I scan in, I can create a page that shows contributors to the site. With the digital audio capture software in Windows, I create short audio dialogues to illustrate concepts like how to handle an objection in a sales call. Threaded discussion group pages can be created, or you can use the collaboration features of your Intranet or Lotus Notes. You can also create online chatrooms with instant messenger programs available for free, or you can create a more elaborate virtual meeting room on Web sites like Placeware (*placeware.com*) and WebEx (*webex.com*).

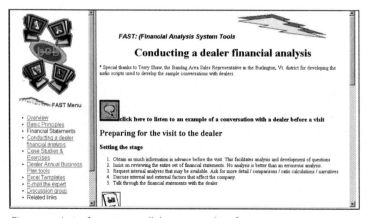

Figure 9.1 A site for training, collaboration, and performance support.

The sites develop and morph over time to address current interests and needs of the user group. I create simple instructions on how to upload and download files like word processed documents, spreadsheet templates, and even short audio clips; these get collected onto a "latest and greatest downloads" page. My clients create incentives to share information through online exposure, small gifts, or modest bonuses. You might tempt a writer or university professor to be an online contributor and mentor by offering real-world case studies and feedback from users.

Would you surprise your managers or sponsors if you told them you could get an online learning and performance support site up and running by the end of the week? If you can get your organization's Web master, a couple of content experts, and some potential learners together in a room with a computer for two days, you can do it.

What you create will not be a "course," and it's probably not appropriate to call it Web-based training. It is better than that. It's not going to be expensive, it's not going to go out of date, and you will be able to confirm its results directly by capturing the online discussions.

As you develop these bytes of training and information, design the site so that it's easily downloaded and displayed on a PDA. Create audio in MP3 files that can be played on a portable player. Attach small word processing files or spreadsheets that can be used immediately on a PDA. Think small, think fast, and think portable.

BEING USER AND CREATOR: INTEGRATING MOBILE DEVICES IN YOUR PROFESSIONAL TOOLKIT

All too often, training, information technology, and communication professionals are great at recommending new solutions to their clients but do not become users themselves. Most instructional designers have never taken a Web-based training course themselves, even though they may develop them regularly, and, sadly, sometimes even people in IT and communications are like the proverbial shoemaker's children: They don't have the budget or time to explore new technologies.

Fortunately, mobile devices are both less expensive and easier to use than many of the learning technologies introduced over the past two decades like videodisc, teleconferencing, and even CD-ROMs. Since they are meant to be consumer devices, they can be readily purchased and operated. Creating custom applications may take a bit more time and skill, but once you have created or licensed an authoring platform, there are a variety of applications that you can deploy. Not only can you use mobile devices for training, but you can also use them as a marketing and demonstration tool for your services.

UP CLOSE

Interview with
Edward Prentice III, President,
Centrax Corporation, Chicago, Illinois

A number of training program vendors are already committed to using mobile platforms for their products. These companies, like Centrax, whose initiatives are described below, are good models for using new technologies both as an end-product and also as marketing tools.

Briefly describe what device you are using and what the applications consist of. Our products TrainingBYTEs and PromoBYTEs are used for e-learning and e-marketing [see Figure 9.2]. We have developed a number of e-learning programs that provide training for field-related issues such as equipment repair and on-site safety training. Until PDA technology came along, these training modules were delivered via laptops or desktop PCs. We reformatted our products to work on three main models that use the Microsoft Pocket PC operating system: Compaq-IPAQ, HP-Jornada, and Casio-Cassiopeia. We chose the Pocket PC operating system because we needed to take training beyond text-based training programs. We have our own sales demonstrations as well as educational programs for our clients with whom we are using these devices.

The training programs will mainly consist of short-format content that can be efficiently used in the field for equipment training or sales presentations.

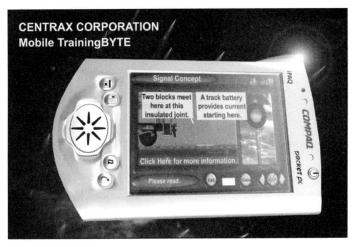

Figure 9.2 Mobile TrainingBYTE. (Courtesy Centrax Corporation, www.centrax.com)

What got you started in using the mobile device or devices?
Centrax decided to move its TrainingBYTEs and PromoBYTEs
applications to portable devices due to client needs. Many training
programs are needed in the field, and it is not conducive to take
laptops to certain environments. There is also the issue of the
boot-up time for laptops versus the "instant-on" capability of
PDAs. Converting our TrainingBYTE application was a seamless
migration to PDAs. We have an ASP [application service provider]
service called the Centrax Customizable TrainingBYTE [CCT]
Service. This service allows our clients to make changes to
TrainingBYTEs using an Internet-based customization site—
custom programmed for their organization—before they download them. We have applied this service to mobile learning as well.

**Explain how the application is used. Who are the users,
and what is the setting?** Internally, our sales staff uses PDAs
for sales presentations. The setting can be anywhere due to the
portable nature of PDAs. Staff members are able to be on an air-
plane and show a presentation to a prospect without having to
boot up their laptop. Our clients use the PDAs for employee or
customer training. In most cases, they are purchasing PDAs and
issuing them on a loaner basis. The TrainingBYTEs cover areas
ranging from process and safety training on a plant floor to
repairing cell site equipment in the field.

What have been the business or productivity results? Our
sales staff has been able to close deals for our service in a matter of days. When using our PDAs for a presentation, the proof
of concept for mobile learning is easy to convey. For example,
we are working with a large financial institution that wants to
use the PDAs combined with a New Employee Orientation
TrainingBYTE. This will increase interviewing process productivity in areas that have high turnover such as teller hiring. The
organization can have ten to fifteen PDAs at the front desk versus a room full of PCs. The PDAs can then be wirelessly connected to a server in order to download survey or questionnaire
information from interviewees. They can sit in the lobby and
use the PDA devices. This cuts back on paperwork and keying
in information from printed sheets.

**Explain exactly how the application is created and then
used by the end user. What software or programming lan-**

guage is used, who is on the team that creates this, and how does the user get it and manipulate it on his or her device? Centrax takes content from our clients' existing courses and produces TrainingBYTEs. Our core competencies stem from our roots in the multimedia and educommerce/edutainment industries. Our proficiencies in three-dimensional character and product animation, engaging graphic design, and advanced programming enable us to produce effective Mobile TrainingBYTEs for our clients. Our team uses software from Microsoft, such as Visual Basic, Visual C++, and SQL, and Macromedia [Flash] software tools to develop Mobile TrainingBYTEs. From a delivery to the end-user standpoint, we provide consultation to organizations in order to select the best technology. One solution is for the users to download the TrainingBYTE to their desktops and then synchronize the PDA while it is in its cradle. We have custom PDA software installation tools that perform this process while the PDA is connected. We can also set up a server where the TrainingBYTEs (and data transfer from TrainingBYTEs) can be accessed by the PDA wirelessly.

For most clients, we use wireless LAN [WLAN] technology for distributing TrainingBYTEs to the PDAs within an office or plant environment. Each PDA will have a WLAN card for sending and receiving information to the server. We also have server and PDA software tools that are necessary for synchronization when using WLANs. Most clients prefer this in order to eliminate the PDA cradle synchronization step.

How long does it typically take to design and deploy such an application? Our production staff can develop portable TrainingBYTEs in two to four weeks depending on the complexity of the program. If in the original preliminary analysis of an e-learning course, it is determined that segments of content will be needed in the field, we will format the content as a "Mobile" TrainingBYTE.

With our ASP [CCT Service—Centrax Customizable Training-BYTE Service] model, a client can go online and make changes to its TrainingBYTE over the Internet in a matter of minutes. For example, a salesperson can access the company's CTS site from a hotel room and make changes to a sales presentation before downloading it to his or her PDA or laptop. The same presentation can be on the laptop for a boardroom presentation or on the PDA for a park bench presentation!

What were the biggest challenges or unexpected hurdles? We spent the most time designing a TrainingBYTE and interface template that will be viewable within the small window size. As we developed our vertical application services, we needed to build in solutions for battery charging process training and plans for synchronization with a centralized database. Each client usually has a different network setup that requires analysis and proper selection of software tools that will enable PDAs to sync with a central server.

What are your future plans for mobile devices applications for training or business communications with your employees and customers? We are currently developing vertical applications with our Mobile TrainingBYTEs. For example, we are developing a series of TrainingBYTEs for the American Medical Association to be made available for download by its members. One module is on osteoporosis training for physicians. Physicians will be able to log on to the AMA site and download TrainingBYTEs that cover specific medical issues. They will then be able to view the training programs on the PDA, which is more convenient than sitting at a desk or carrying a laptop computer around.

We will also be developing off-the-shelf programs for individual users to purchase on our *TrainingBYTE.com* site. The first module is on carpal tunnel syndrome prevention. Other areas will include time management and personal health–related topics.

What advice would you give to fellow training, business performance, and communications professionals with regard to getting into the use of mobile devices? First, make sure that the content is suitable for the device. Training programs that are long and text heavy will not work efficiently due to the small screen size of PDAs. Second, get the appropriate technical assistance on the front end before investing in a large number of PDAs or connectivity software. Third, there is a need to study how the PDAs will be used based on audience and environment. There may be a need for industrial versions of PDAs if they will be used in harsh locations. Last but not least, make friends with your IT staff!

INITIATING MOBILE LEARNING: STRATEGIC CONSIDERATIONS

By now, you may be fairly convinced that mobile learning technologies have a role in your professional practice. But it is likely that you are not the sole decision maker. You may be able to go out and buy a Pocket PC or MP3 player for yourself, but if you are thinking about deploying one of these technologies within your organization or recommending one to a client, you must have buy-in. Mobile technologies are no different from many other information technologies; to get them approved and implemented, a number of stakeholders need to be involved and convinced. There's no surefire way to do this, but there are models that you can use.

PROPOSING SOLUTIONS AND GETTING BUY-IN

One of the best ways to start a new initiative like mobile learning is to garner a cross-functional team to study needs and do an economic analysis and recommendation. Because mobile technologies inextricably link training, performance management, communications, and information technologies, coordinating the effort across organizational silos is crucial. Above all, getting executive buy-in and input from operating units is critical, because any new technology implementation should start with business goals, not with the technology.

One of the most effective efforts in looking at not only new technologies but also the new approaches to communication and learning that technologies bring was a task group called FutureCom at a restaurant chain for which I was a consultant. The group assembled a team composed of representatives from employee relations, communications, information technologies, and the various operating units to develop a vision for future communication within the organization. I was brought in as a "communications futurist" to offer new ideas and facilitate the process. I recommend this kind of collaborative effort, even though nobody likes to form or sit on another committee. A typical task force should have the following members:

- ❐ Executive sponsor—responsible for making the investment decision. This person is usually a high-ranking executive who ensures that the team has the budget and support necessary to conduct the study.

- ❐ Team leader—the committee chair, responsible for overall project management and assembly and writing of the business case.

- ❐ Business champions—various representatives from major operating units and departments (staff and line) who identify strategic goals for the organization and understand the business.

- ❐ Learning and communication architects—professionals from training, performance improvement, and internal and external communications departments.

- ❐ Technology manager—an expert in identifying the technologies and solutions that can achieve the strategic goals, typically from the company's IT department.

- ❐ Solution consultant—typically an outside consultant with expertise in applying new technologies to business problems and who is not biased toward or identified with any particular vendor or hardware solution.

- ❐ Financial analyst—an expert in finance who can do the economic analyses needed to make recommendations and show potential return on investment.

❏ Benchmarkers—outside colleagues in similar businesses who have experience in implementing the solutions you're considering.

I use a consulting model called HICCUP—a funny name for a powerful process to address business needs and find solutions with the following five steps:

1. Identify one or more *Hot Items*—business needs that affect the financial, social, and cultural goals of the organizations.

2. Identify *Consequences* of those problems and needs.

3. Analyze the *Causes* of the problem.

4. *Uncover* opportunities by envisioning what the situation would look like if the problem were remedied or if some new opportunity were possible.

5. Brainstorm *Possibilities*—specific solutions that are available and might bring the desirable future state into reality.

An example of using the model is presented in Figure 9.3.

MAKING IT HAPPEN: USING RAPID PROTOTYPING

One powerful approach to implementing new technologies is to do rapid prototyping. The problem with pitching new technologies to executives, sponsors, and end users is that you are probably talking about things that they cannot even imagine. So in the words of a famous ad, "just do it!"

Almost everybody's budget has room for the purchase of an MP3 player, a pocket computer, or a digital camera, and almost every organization has an intranet and e-mail. Go out and buy one of these devices, and first see what you can

Five-Step (HICCUP) System Diagnostic Model

Hot Items What problems or unattained goals significantly impact the organization's success? Examples: Slow communication to employees impedes motivation and feeds the rumor mill; the product development cycle is too long, etc.

Consequences: What do you think are some of the results of this? How does it affect the performance of the organization? How does this impact the long-term valuation of the organization from a prospective buyer's or stockholder's perspective?

Causes: Why do you think this situation exists? Are some people actually benefiting from the current state? Are people aware of the current situation and its consequences? Are people aware of alternative ways to manage the situation? Is communication or learning just too difficult and are our current tools not effective and efficient?

Uncover Opportunity: If this situation were different, how would it improve our position as individuals and as an organization? What would it look like if we magically could correct this? What resources would it make available for other opportunities? What would it look like if we had a magic "black box" that could provide communications and knowledge support?

Possibilities: What would it take to change the situation? What kinds of technologies are available today? Who could implement them? Who's done it before? What's the expected return on investment? What would success look like in the short term and the long term?

Figure 9.3 HICCUP model for developing a business case.

download for free from existing sources. Next, investigate how you might apply it in your own organization. But don't try to take on the world. The question I ask my clients is, "What can we do in one day?" I have run workshops where we take some existing content, format it in HTML for a Web page, or export an electronic slide show to HTML format, and create instant information nuggets and job aids. Try to identify an annoying problem or persistent information need and develop an application to solve it. Use it yourself. Then try it out on a group of innovators. Every organization has a cadre of innovators who like to test out new technologies. Do not limit your trial to them. Identify people who have the business need and see if your solution works for them. Listen to their experiences; it's important to identify both the risks and the benefits of implementing any new hardware or software.

Once you have one or two simple applications developed that seem to have support, roll out these success stories to the rest of the organization and see who wants to bite. You may want to budget for a set of units that can be borrowed, or you may be able to convince a vendor to provide demonstration units while you're considering a widespread implementation.

MANAGING MOBILE LEARNING AND PERFORMANCE TOOLS: ETHICAL CONSIDERATIONS

It would not be responsible to tout the benefits of mobile technologies for learning and performance without talking frankly about the possible risks and even abuses of their implementation. As a manager or advocate of new technologies, it is essential to develop policies and communications that limit possible undesirable side effects:

❒ *Loss of privacy.* As mobile devices incorporate built-in tracking (as with GPS systems and new cell phones with the ability to identify user's locations), many people fear a loss of privacy. Does your employer track your every move? Are all your communications recorded and available for review? To some extent, many of these issues have been faced in the implementation of e-mail. Now, most employees understand that nothing they write using a company's e-mail system is private; in fact, no actions that they take on an employer-owned computer or network such as surfing Web sites or saving memos on a hard drive are exempt from examination. However, even more tracking can lead to abuses, and what is done with that information can lead at the very least to misunderstanding and mistrust.

❒ *Stressful work conditions.* When employees feel like they are "never off"—that is, they are available to be called at any time on their cell phones and they are expected to be taking training and communicating 24 hours a day, 7 days a week—the conditions are there for very stressful and undesirable impacts on their personal and work lives. Being monitored and having even more messages to respond to and information to learn can lead to decreased rather than increased performance and a very unhealthy corporate culture. Adding only one more new technology to learn and take care of is a stressor.

❒ *Deskilling work.* Although it is certainly nice to provide job aids to people to minimize errors and provide performance support, we need to be careful not to turn people into robots who are expected just to follow instructions doled out to them on their computer devices. By taking the skill, spontaneity, and creativity out of jobs, we decrease motivation and make people overly reliant on new technologies rather than their own intelligence and goodwill.

❑ *Manipulation and interception of data.* As more information about people and more critical company information are stored and transmitted, there is the obvious threat to the integrity of the data. Is it possible for someone to hack data, jeopardizing individuals' or the organization's critical information? Can competitors intercept sensitive and confidential messages? Who has access to private messaging and personal information such as test scores, whereabouts, performance indicators, or even health, family, and financial records?

We have all seen examples, from large-scale public disasters to personal annoyances, of information technologies that went wrong. We get in-baskets full of junk e-mails, hours or years of lost work when systems crash, an inability to work when the infrastructure goes down, and attacks on personal and organizational property by hackers. As we implement new technologies, we need to make sure that we do not inadvertently revert to the worst examples of scientific management where people were supervised and rewarded by time-and-motion efficiency models. We also need to ensure that we do not become overly dependent on technologies and lose our ability to function when the inevitable crashes occur. Most of all, we need to design systems that amplify rather than diminish individual creativity, diversity, expertise, and connectedness. Implemented correctly, mobile technologies can make people free, powerful, and flexible. They can increase social capital by making it easier for people to meet, interact, and develop strong bonds.

It's up to you to make it happen—both the technological *and* the social vision.

Index

About the Author

DIANE GAYESKI, Ph.D., is widely acknowledged as a leader in using new communication and learning technologies to improve workplace performance. Since 1980, she has led more than three hundred projects for clients worldwide, helping them to learn about and apply innovative concepts and media for training, employee communication, collaboration, and performance support. As CEO of Gayeski Analytics, she conducts communication and training system audits, develops strategies and prototypes, and leads workshops and executive briefings. She is the author of twelve books and has been featured in numerous publications, including the *Wall Street Journal, Training, Communication World, Training and Development,* and *Performance Improvement.* She is also professor of organizational communication, learning, and design at Ithaca College, Ithaca, New York.